GOOD OLD GEORGE
The Life of George Lansbury

George Lansbury led the Labour Party in the crisis years of the early 1930s. Throughout that time, he campaigned with passionate sincerity for a just society — as he had done for many years before, as Poor Law Guardian, rebel councillor, socialist preacher, journalist, editor of the *Daily Herald* and MP. He was a working man, and he spoke his message of social justice in words that ordinary people could understand. He sought practical ways to relieve poverty. To the end of his days, he lived modestly in the East End of London, and his home was open to his neighbours and constituents.

His sincerity and commitment to the cause of social justice have made him what A.J.P. Taylor has described as 'the most loveable figure in modern politics'. But Lansbury himself would probably have appreciated more the chants of children whenever he appeared at schools or playgrounds: 'Good old George.'

Bob Holman's biography sheds new light not only on his political career and socialist commitment, but also on the sincere Christian faith that inspired and maintained him.

BOB HOLMAN brings to his topic a rare combination of scholarly and practical understanding. For several years he lectured and researched at the universities of Birmingham and Glasgow before moving to the Chair of Social Administration at Bath. Later he left academic life to initiate a community project for the Children's Society and he now serves as a neighbourhood worker on the large council estate of Easterhouse in Glasgow, dealing with social issues at the grass-roots level.

TO JOAN PARK
Christian, socialist and friend

GOOD OLD GEORGE
The Life of George Lansbury

Bob Holman

A LION PAPERBACK
Oxford · Batavia · Sydney

Copyright © 1990 Robert Holman

Published by
Lion Publishing plc
Sandy Lane West, Oxford, England
ISBN 0 7459 1574 4
Albatross Books Pty Ltd
PO Box 320, Sutherland, NSW 2232, Australia
ISBN 0 7324 0275 1

First published 1990

British Library Cataloguing in Publication Data

Holman, Bob
  Good old George : the life of George Lansbury.
  1. Great Britain. Politics. Lansbury, George, 1859–1940
  I. Title
  941.085092

  ISBN 0-7459-1574-4

Printed and bound in Britain

CONTENTS

FOREWORD

No British politician in this century has walked the high wire strung between utopianism and pragmatism with greater skill or to more effect than George Lansbury. That, and much more, is brought out in Bob Holman's much needed biography. Here we step back and become part of George Lansbury's world while at the same time gleaning the big lessons from his life.

Balance is as important in politics as it is to the trapeze artist. For the radical politician a balance needs to be held between, on the one hand, utopian vision and, on the other, a list of bread-and-butter reforms which can be realized in the foreseeable future. Both stances are important. To be concerned only with the immediate issues, unguided by utopian ideals, leaves the politician at the mercy of every opinion poll finding. But utopianism too is open to a subtle corruption. It can provide a mere high-sounding platform for gesture politics if it is not accompanied by practical programmes mapping out the first steps along the road to perfection. George Lansbury's life is an exemplary study of this necessary political balance and how it needs constantly to be struck.

Early on Christianity became, and remained, the corner-stone of Lansbury's utopian vision. His refreshingly simple stance on God the Father, with each one of us being children of God, led naturally to the belief that we are all part of one family. From that simple corpus of views sprang a programme with revolutionary implications. Whatever our particular gifts and distinguishing marks these differences are small compared to our equality as children of God. Here at one swoop George had a view not only on why major differences in income should not be tolerated, but why life opportunities should be made freely available to all. Lansbury's programme to achieve a society where co-operation and fellowship are dominant values would today be received with more scepticism than it was during

7

most of George's lifetime. At a time when most of Eastern Europe is throwing off the yoke of state socialism and the inefficiency of state economic planning, few will now embrace this particular approach.

Yet while the programme remains suspect George's objectives remain as important as ever. But those objectives can only be achieved if the Left begins with a more accurate understanding about what underlies personal motivation. As well as the noble aims, we need to take on board and give due weight to self-interest. This is far too important a personal motive force to be ignored as it has been in most socialist and Christian left-wing thinking. Similarly, today many Christians and socialists would be critical of the simplest view of condemning outright profit and the profit motive, while seeing this as all part of a wicked capitalist plot. Profits are, or should be, to markets what lubricating oil is to an engine. The crucial questions, to me anyway, are not ones concerned with a simple blanket condemnation of profits as such but the questions about to whom these profits accrue and within what moral framework does a market system operate.

I suspect that Lansbury would be quick in responding to this line in argument. Much the strongest card he would play would be on the failure of socialism in Eastern Europe. While now he would see, as Bob Holman suggests, the degree of generous naïvety in which he held the Soviet system, he could point to a consistent belief throughout his life that socialism could only be maintained if it was freely embraced. He would add more of course. Socialism can only be spread and sustained if its beliefs are lived by socialists. And in Lansbury's view, that sustenance can only come from a living Christian faith. At a number of points in the story Bob Holman beautifully knits together the interrelationship of the two powerful beliefs in Lansbury's life. On some occasions it is difficult to distinguish whether Lansbury is talking as a Christian or as a socialist. That, George might well have added, is how it inevitably must be.

It is when socialism is taken away from how individuals should be treated and rooted into a political programme that it risks being caught in a time warp. For part of this story it can appear that Lansbury equated votes for women with socialism. But it was rather the inequality of treatment meted out to women, and in those days to many men as well, all of whom are equal in God's sight, that Lansbury deplored. His particular programme to redress these political inequalities was the widening of the franchise. The job of the Christian Left, if it is to live, is to deduce what today's programme should be on the basis of the obvious needs we see around us, combined with an understanding of the great Christian verities. Indeed these verities will help shape what we see as needs.

It is surprising, and perhaps equally disturbing, that so many of the most simple lessons Lansbury tried to teach are still be be learnt. Nowhere have I seen a better undermining of the idea which sees Christianity only in terms of personal morality than in this biography. Lansbury's own life showed that Christianity is very much a creed which rules a person's daily conduct. But Christianity must have an equally dominant social role as well. What are we to think of a Christianity which cares everything for an individual's soul but nothing much for the material well-being of the body in which that soul lives? Lansbury's sacramental view of the body as a temple in which the redeeming Spirit of God can live made for a comprehensive view of the Christian domain.

Lansbury's great 'failure' entails an important lesson. A respectable case can still be mounted for Lansbury's pacifism which not only spanned World War I but which extended up to and into World War II. The role of the prophet is never more needed than in the darkest hour but just because the hour is dark does not necessarily mean all prophecy will be correct. What Lansbury's views needed, as did those of most Christian leaders at this time, including William Temple, was the balancing influence of Reinhart Niebuhr's theology. The full nature of man, including our sinful side, needs to become part of our understanding. It's not one, of course, that should stunt our vision, but it must be there, particularly when we face an evil as big as that posed by Nazism. George's trips to plead with the Führer show that he, like many, had no idea of the extent of the evil that he felt so confident could be dealt with by a simple Christian apologia.

Lansbury here was caught, as were so many Christians, by the one-sided enthusiasm of the incarnational school which dominated British theology during the last quarter of the nineteenth century and which spilled over into this century. While the inadequacies of this theology were there to see when the First World War burst ruthlessly upon the scene, many of the inter-war leaders, especially those on the Left, and Christians too, had been grounded in a somewhat naïve faith. Yet, against this view, it must be added that the farther we move away from the buildup to the Second World War, the more important it appears that some bright soul should have kept alive a literal interpretation of the gospel.

I will detain the reader to make one other point. Another of

Lansbury's lessons is still to be learnt by most of us. George's almost bitter condemnation of Toynbee Hall and its like, and the symbolism of its middle-class imperialism towards the poor, is scathingly dealt with here. This judgment surely needs modifying. To have a place where the technocrat such as Beveridge learnt firsthand about unemployment, albeit that of others, the need for labour exchanges (now called job centres), a national system of insurance to guard against destitution and the workhouse, as well as gaining the expertise to draft an economic policy to counter cyclical swings in economic activity, is surely worth something. Similarly, to have grounded Left politicians in some of the realities of life as it affects the least privileged is not to be sneered at. Rightly, as is cited here, the work of Mary Hughes and her Dew Drop Inn is to be saluted, but does praise here have to be exclusively at the expense of others doing different work? Surely the task of building a more just society is so difficult and so precarious that all these skills and abilities should be welcomed and supported even if they should fall short of ideal practice.

Here is illustrated, better than anywhere, how frail many of us on the Left are. Few can aspire to the Lansbury tradition of so truly living out our faith. Few have the strength that Lansbury showed or the integrity that Bob Holman practices in the selfless way he has added his talents into building a common good. What we can do is draw strength from yesterday's and today's prophets, and this brings me back to the role of the moral utopian visionary who is also a daily worker in the vineyard. We can thank God for the likes of George Lansbury and Bob Holman who in their own ways bring alive the Christian faith by the very fact of living.

FRANK FIELD MP

Chairperson of the House of Commons
Select Committee on Social Services

PREFACE

George Lansbury died during the Second World War. At the time, Britain was concentrating on national survival and hence his death never received the usual attention given to a former leader of a major political party. Yet he was a remarkable and inspiring man and I hope, in this book, to bring him back to public recognition.

The main sources for the study have been the Lansbury Collection at the London School of Economics and Political Science and files at Bancroft Road Library in Tower Hamlets, not far from Lansbury's old home in Bow Road. The former contains Lansbury's personal papers, newspaper reports about him and many articles by him. The latter has further personal documents, local newspaper reports and photographs. Apart from an early memoir by his son, Edgar, and a biography by his son-in-law, Raymond Postgate — written over forty years ago — there are no books about Lansbury. However, he wrote many books and pamphlets himself and I have had access to most, if not all, of these. In addition, I recorded interviews with three people who knew him well: Michael Foot MP, Viscount Tonypandy (formerly George Thomas MP), and the Rev. Lord Donald Soper. I also met Professor William Fishman who knew Lansbury only slightly but who has an immense knowledge of Lansbury's East End. I received written comments from a number of Lansbury's relatives, particularly Mr Terry Lansbury, Mrs Esme Whiskin, Professor John Postgate and Mr Richmond Postgate. I also had letters from others who knew him: Mrs Marjorie Pinhorn, Mrs Rose Rosamund, Mrs G. Wootton, and the Rev. Allan Harling. Mr Geoffrey Goodman and the Rev. Clive Barrett sent valuable comments. I am grateful to them all for their contribution.

I also appreciate the encouragement of my publishers who decided that the story of George Lansbury was worth telling.

In his books, Lansbury went out of his way to thank all the people who helped him in his work. I must do the same. My wife, Annette, and our daughter and son, Ruth and David, must feel that George Lansbury is another member of our family. I thank them for welcoming him. My friend, Mrs Audrey Browne, kindly offered to type the manuscript free of charge. I am grateful to Frank Field MP for writing a foreword. I approached him because he, like Lansbury, is a politician of integrity and one who has put the cause of poor people before his own advancement. Finally, the book is dedicated to Mrs Joan Park. I knew Joan in the years when, as a lone parent, she raised a large family. Despite her low income, she remained a hardworking activist within the Labour Party, a faithful church member and a good and generous friend. George Lansbury always felt most at home with people like Joan Park.

Bob Holman
Easterhouse, Glasgow
February 1990

1
THE FORMATIVE YEARS

A small boy watched flames engulfing a row of wooden dwellings. The huts were the temporary homes of railway workers who moved from place to place as the Victorian railways were extended. He had seen such buildings reduced to ashes on previous occasions but this time the homeless included his aunt and cousins.

Fires were bad enough; tunnel collapses were even worse. The boy's uncle was one of the victims when hundreds of tons of earth buried some labourers alive. He witnessed the subsequent funeral when the dead were carried in rough coffins by their workmates.

These incidents had a profound influence on the boy. He began to question why human beings should be treated so badly by employers who placed their own material gain over the safety and lives of their employees. Further, his acquaintance with death convinced him — for some reason that he could not fathom — that death was not the end. He later wrote, 'From my first thinking moments I believed in life after death — that is, my faith is absolute in the words "there is no death". '[1]

The boy was George Lansbury. In his early years, political life was dominated by Disraeli and Gladstone. The Labour Party had not even been formed, yet one day George was to become its leader. The same boy, who rarely went to church but who possessed an instinctive belief in life after death, was to become a prominent Christian whose 'voice was more influential in the Church than the average bishop's'.[2]

George Lansbury was born on 21 February 1859, in a Suffolk toll house. His place of birth could have been almost anywhere, for his father was employed as a timekeeper with a firm of railway contractors. The Lansbury family moved with the navvies as they constructed and repaired railway lines. Their homes were the wooden huts so vulnerable to destruction by fire.

Little is known about his father, George Lansbury senior. The fact that he was a heavy drinker may have contributed to George's lifelong teetotalism. In his autobiography, Lansbury speaks more about his mother, Anne. She too drank heavily but also gave her children much affection. Whatever the drinking habits of George and Anne Lansbury, they must have been resourceful people. Mr Lansbury held a responsible post and Mrs Lansbury coped with four (and eventually nine) children while constantly moving from place to place. Later the moves became less frequent when Mr Lansbury set himself up as a self-employed unloader of railway trucks and barges and the family settled into a house in Sydenham. George recorded one of his earliest memories from this period. His mother had been knocked down — he did not say how — and suffered a broken leg. He wrote, 'It was then we learned how the poor help the poor,' for it was neighbours who nursed the mother back to health and who looked after the young Lansbury's.[3]

While at Sydenham, probably aged eight, George started school. There was no compulsory education; school was the front room of a cottage and the teacher was an old lady. The school had few materials and pupils sat on the floor. Nonetheless, George was taught the alphabet and some arithmetic.

Father's business must have prospered, for he invited a brother to join him and the family moved to Greenwich where George met people from a different social class. He later recorded that 'we had learned all about our duty to our neighbour and ordering ourselves lowly and reverently to our betters: but until we got to Greenwich the "betters" had not come our way, except in the form of the parson'.[4] Now the Lansbury's were invited to tea with the manager who controlled the contracts given to loaders. Mrs Lansbury washed and brushed her children and warned them to be on their very best behaviour.

They enjoyed a gorgeous tuck-in, but the highlight was the presence of a piano. They had heard of such an instrument but never seen one, let alone touched one. George could not resist pushing down his finger and making a note. His mother instantly rebuked him. Happily, the lady of the house was not annoyed and allowed George to run his finger along the keyboard, an experience which sent a thrill right through him.

At Greenwich, George heard more about politics, for his mother was sympathetic to radical movements. He also witnessed the uproar and rowdiness of the 1868 election in Greenwich when the returning of David Salomans did much to confirm the right of Jews to sit in parliament.

Towards the end of 1868, the family moved yet again, briefly to Bethnal Green and then to Whitechapel. Here George's schooling became more intermittent, and at age eleven George left school having found a job in the office of a coal merchant. It was to be short lived, for he ran away from home and spent a period in Herefordshire, where he worked as a potboy in a pub. However, within a year he was not only back home but also back at school.

St Mary's School in Whitechapel consisted of one large room with classes in each corner and one in the middle. George admired the headmaster, Michael Apted, and from that time on became an avid reader, being enthralled by Jules Verne adventure stories and later by Tennyson, Browning and William Morris. Lansbury also recorded that it was while at St Mary's that he organized his first campaign with a petition pleading that the pupils be allowed playtime. The request was granted. Outside of school, he also seemed full of high spirits and Postgate described him as follows:

careering round the streets, playing football — which largely
consisted in fighting and kicking other players — leaping from
barge to barge on the Thames, and once at least nearly meeting
death in the water: he showed in these years a boyish exuberance
which he never quite lost.[5]

In spite of his exuberance, George possessed a serious side which prevented him following the downward path of some of his mates. Years later, when elected to the Commons in 1910, he received a letter from such a friend by then in New Zealand. Thomas Tillmoor wrote:

You went the right road I went the wrong. You sought everything
that would improve your character and mind . . . You went to
the lads' institute, I went to the Pavilion Theatre almost nightly.
I learned to drink beer, you escaped, thank God.

In 1873, at the age of fourteen, George left school for good. He did a number of jobs before joining his father and brother James in the family business of unloading coal from trains and barges. Mr

Lansbury died in 1875 and the two brothers took over the contract with the Great Eastern Railway. For a while they were supporting the whole family until their mother eventually remarried.

Coal heaving was hard work and probably contributed to the development of George's powerful physique. The job also frequently entailed night shifts, so the teenage George would labour from 1 a.m. to 7 or 8 a.m., go home for a rest, and then watch cricket or occasionally attend the debates in the House of Commons. The unloading also took him into the world of railwaymen and he formed friendships with drivers, guards, platelayers, greasers and shunters employed at the goods depot at Bishopsgate. The Great Eastern Railway refused to supply poles with which to uncouple waggons and George had known four men who were crushed to death as they uncoupled by hand. Again, he was observing how cheaply the life of working-class people was held in the quest for private profit. Yet he had no thoughts of a political career and would have been amazed to have realized that fifty years later he would be a leader in the same House of Commons where he went to listen.

If the seeds of George Lansbury's later political beliefs were being sown at this time, so too were those of his Christian faith. The impression is sometimes given that Christianity enjoyed a golden age in Victorian Britain. In fact, although church-going was a popular middle-class habit, the church historian Stephen Mayor points out that the second half of the nineteenth century was accompanied by 'repeated laments at the decline of the church and above all at the absence of the working classes'.[6]

George's early awareness of the closeness of death had sparked off his belief in a life eternal. However, his parents do not seem to have been regular church-goers and George later stated that Sunday School had little effect on him. Far from coming under strong Christian influences, he began listening to atheists. Attacks on the authenticity of the Bible were commonplace, and during the last quarter of the nineteenth century, as Mayor explains, 'the exponents of scepticism were beginning to address themselves chiefly to the working classes'.[7] They argued that religion, particularly Christianity, upheld the existing social order by teaching the poor to humbly accept their poverty as the will of God. George Lansbury went to hear Charles Bradlaugh and other leading rationalist figures and he expressed admiration for their courage when they continued despite some rough handling from the crowds and little protection from the police.

Just when religion meant least to Lansbury, he came under the influence of the Rev. Fenwick Kitto, the vicar of Whitechapel. It is not clear how the two met, although Lansbury links the initial encounter with the death of his father. Probably Kitto took the funeral service. Kitto was a high churchman who restored chanting and ceremonial to the parish services. However, it was not the services or Kitto's intellectual prowess which impressed the young Lansbury. Rather, as Lansbury himself explained, 'nobody has ever had quite the same influence, in a way it is not possible to explain, on my wife and myself as he did. He entered into our lives, teaching us mainly by example.'[8]

Those words, 'He entered into our lives', are a beautiful testimony to an ordinary clergyman whose name would now be almost forgotten save for the fact that he touched the life of a man who was to become a national figure. It appears that Kitto took an enormous interest in and gave much time to the working-class and often very poor young people of his parish. He discussed with them what they should do when their employers expected them to lie to customers. He taught them that Christianity was practical in its expression and had to be displayed at home and work. He invited them to meals at the rectory and stimulated the bonds of friendship between them.

Lansbury was confirmed at the parish church. To him the ceremony was no mere form of words. He was now a Christian believer whose faith was to affect deeply all that he did. At this juncture, the nature of his faith is best revealed in a number of letters — happily preserved — which George wrote to his closest friend, Wait Sewell. They both became Sunday school teachers and, on one occasion in 1877 when Wait was away for some reason, George wrote to him that the meeting went quite well until one of the boys cheeked a teacher 'so he boxed his ears and the boy had wanted to fight. It was quite a tragic scene ending with the boy walking out of the school.' The letter reveals that Victorian Sunday schools were not always quiet, well-behaved affairs but could be difficult to control. But George's sympathies somehow remained even with rowdy pupils. Probably he recalled what he was like at their age.

Throughout these years, the teenage Lansbury's Christian faith remained strong. Wait, however, went through periods of religious lows and, in a letter dated 31 October 1878, George counselled him:

17

I think that when you have accepted Christ you repent of your sins by that act. You show that you mean by His grace to lead a better, purer and holier life. I do not think that we have any right after we are converted to be sorry; we should rather be rejoicing at having such an unspeakable gift in your possession.

George clearly had a great concern for Wait and their friendship was to continue for many years. He was also concerned about the boys at the Sunday school and appears to have given them his time both inside and outside the church. Later, in 1884, a young man named Alf Everitt wrote to Lansbury with these words:

I sincerely hope I shall always endeavour to live up to the principles which you have so earnestly taught us on so many pleasant Sunday afternoons . . . I can truthfully say you have left your mark on a good many of us in the class, which is apparent in the greater restraint and more open mindedness shown between one another.'

It is important to note that Lansbury's Christianity preceded his socialism, for the latter was to spring largely from his understanding of the former. At this time, Lansbury knew little about socialism and had no thoughts about entering politics. Yet, in one way, his new-found Christianity was to prepare him for political involvement. Politics entails public speaking, and as Lansbury threw himself into Christian service so he had to learn to address meetings large and small. He chaired meetings at the Band of Hope and participated in debates at the Whitechapel Church Young Men's Association. Interestingly, at one debate he spoke on the subject of Peace Against War. These were the years when popular support was backing the British forces as they fought in Afghanistan and as they extended the empire in Africa. Yet already Lansbury was a pacifist with his opposition to war rooted in his Christianity. By now he was often asked to speak and preach, but talk was not sufficient. In addition, he helped a member of the Society of Friends with the provision of breakfasts on Sunday mornings for about a hundred tramps and casuals and he was increasingly encouraging his railway friends to join a trade union as protection against exploitation by their employer.

Another teacher in the Sunday school was Bessie Brine. She and George had known each other at school and they began to walk out together when he was sixteen and she was fourteen. They had little money to spend on theatres or restaurants, even if they had wanted to. Instead, they worked together in serving others. As well as the Sunday school, they both helped at the Band of Hope where Bessie played the harmonium to songs like

Nail the Cross on the door,
Throw the bottle on the floor

Bessie was probably better educated than George. Certainly, her handwriting is easier to read and she corrected his spelling for many years. Like George she possessed a strong character and was ready to express her views. Fortunately, her opinions usually — but not always — coincided with those of George. They were at one in their Christianity and later were to be at one in their socialism. However, in the 1870s they were more concerned about their love for each other, but the path of true love was not to run smooth. Mr and Mrs Brine considered young Lansbury to be a bit beneath them in the social scale and tried to stop the match. George nicknamed Mr Brine 'the bully', and in a letter to Wait Sewell in 1877, he recounts one row. The Brines had objected to Bessie's new hair-style in which her hair hung down her back. They ordered her to stay indoors but she slipped out and fled to George. He brought her back, when Mrs Brine told him to stop courting her daughter. Bessie then ran off again, in fear, as George put it, 'of that great hulking bully of a father' who had threatened to break her neck. It appears that, later at night, George and his friends did persuade Bessie to return to the Brine household.

Gradually, the Brines accepted George and, in August 1878, he was writing to Wait, 'I have much pleasure in telling you that Bessie is about to buy a large lamp like my mother's. So you see we mean business.' Apparently, the purchase of the lamp signalled the start of the bottom drawer and soon after they became engaged. However, their marriage was delayed by an illness George suffered, the nature of which is not now known. It entailed a lengthy stay in a convalescent home. Thus not only was his pay from work lost but he also had to pay for the convalescence. As a result, George ran into debt which meant that marriage was out of the question. On his return to health, George worked hard, saved hard and paid off what he owed. On 29 May 1880, George aged twenty-one and Bessie aged nineteen were married by the Reverend Kitto at Whitechapel Church.

A year later, George's mother died and the young couple took on the care of George's two youngest brothers. Bessie gave birth to three children of her own — Bessie, Annie and George — in rapid succession, so within a few years George's small earnings were feeding seven mouths. Coping with a large family on little money was to be a feature of Lansbury family life. Yet it never dimmed their happiness. Bessie was never prepared to be the stereotype of the Victorian housewife who had no interests outside the home. Nonetheless, she was a devoted wife and mother who kept the home together despite considerable hardships. George always participated fully in the care of the children. On one occasion, he tried to amuse them by putting on the top hat he had worn for their wedding. For some reason, little Bessie was terrified by the hat so George promptly kicked it, sat on it and destroyed it to prove that it could do no harm. Not least, Bessie and George remained close to each other and he was later to write, 'I am sure our marriage was the most blessed and fortunate thing that ever happened to me.'[9]

In 1884, the Lansbury family left for Australia. Their reason for going to the colonies appears to have been that George was finding it hard to earn a wage sufficient for the family. The coal-loading business had folded and other jobs were difficult to find. So, in May 1884, George and Bessie boarded a four-masted vessel, the *Duke of Devonshire*, taking with them their children and George's twelve-year-old brother whom he described as 'a rather difficult packet to handle at times'.[10] The other brother had found a job and remained in Britain.

The venture got off to a bad start. Contrary to expectations, the ship had no cabins and the 500 emigrants slept in boxes which resembled coffins. In these cramped conditions, Bessie was seasick for nearly all of the eight weeks on board. Food was in short supply and George recorded his thanks to the ship's second engineer and boilermaker who shared their meals with the sick women. Even so, one woman died. Despite the hardships, George enjoyed much of the trip. He took enormous interest in every port of call and made friends with passengers and crew. Twenty years later, the engineer and boilermaker were to help him in his election campaigns. Moreover, he was quick to protest at any exploitation of black people or women. At the Dutch colony of Batavia, he was disgusted at the way in which the Javanese were treated and he had a fierce row with a large Dutchman who was bullying the women who were carrying coal on to the ship.

At last the storms, the sickness, the bullying were over. On a sunny day in July, the ship sailed into Brisbane harbour. Far from being welcomed, the new arrivals were made to feel almost like the convicts who had previously colonized the land. They were marched to the Immigration Home which the Lansbury's compared unfavourably with the British workhouse. The Home was filthy and all the families slept on the floor where great rats roamed. George later wrote, 'Had I been a person who took drink I would have gone out after seeing my wife in bed and got gloriously drunk. A good many men did this and I don't wonder at it.'[11]

If the Lansburys had found Australia the land of opportunity, as so glowingly described in the emigration literature, then they might well have stayed there and Britain would have missed the political impact of George Lansbury. That was not the case. The emigrants had been promised jobs. There were few. George searched every day without success. He approached the local bishop, who was kind but unable to help. After eight weeks, with most of their money gone, he got a job stonebreaking. A better-paid post came up in a slaughterhouse but George gave it up when he discovered that he was expected to work on Sundays. In desperation, he took the family eighty miles to a farm in the wilderness where he obtained a job as a farm servant. The Lansburys lived in what was little more than a hut which was liable to flooding, had periodic visits from snakes, and was a quarter of a mile from drinking water. Moreover, as food had to be purchased from the farmer at his prices, George found that, far from saving money, he was increasingly in debt. Finally, he took the family back to Brisbane where he obtained some casual farm work, helped prepare the Brisbane cricket pitch for a test match with England and then worked delivering parcels. Being both honest and good at handling horses, George did so well in this post that the boss offered him a partnership.

Ironically, just at this juncture, George and Bessie were increasingly worried about the health of their children. They had suffered, particularly from dysentry, and the parents were fearful that they would be added to the numerous deaths among child emigrants. So when a letter arrived from Mr Brine, offering to pay their fares home, they accepted and sailed in May 1885.

In terms of finding a new life in the colonies, the Australian venture was a fiasco. Yet in many ways it turned out to be a turning point for George's whole future. First, he experienced extreme poverty and rejection. True, in Britain he had faced some hardships and short periods out of work, but never before the possibility of never finding a job in an environment where his family might have starved. Even his brief time as a stonebreaker was important, for stonebreaking was the task forced upon paupers in Britain. It left him with raw hands, splitting headaches and earned him a shilling a day. On his return to Britain, Lansbury was to exhibit a deep concern for the unemployed and for the manner in which the Poor Law treated the poor.

The experience also sharpened his political beliefs. In Australia, he met Victorian free enterprise in its purest form. Small private firms competed with each other unhindered by laws or trade unions. Virtually no social services existed to care for the unemployed. These conditions, Lansbury observed, not only allowed employers to exploit workers but also brutalized the workforce as they competed against each other in order to win the wage that might save them from destitution. Later, he wrote this about the men in the slaughterhouse:

> I think they would have been ready to cut each other's throats as easily as they cut up the carcasses of sheep and bullocks. In fact, there seemed no feeling in them, and I could not wonder at it, because they worked at piece rates. Pain and suffering made no appeal to them, economic necessity crushed their better feelings. [12]

Lansbury was by no means a socialist at this stage but his short duration in Australia had served to confirm his early impressions in the railway yard in East London that industry needed to rest on something more noble than an obsession with profit. Most important of all was the fact that Lansbury's anger with the distress imposed upon emigrants was to push him into the world of political action. Up to now, he had been interested in politics, had participated in debates and had visited the House of Commons but he had never been a political activist. After Australia, all was to change.

References

1   G. Lansbury, *My Life*, Constable, 1928, pp. 16–17.

2   R. Postgate, *The Life of George Lansbury*, Longmans, Green & Co., 1951, p. 293.

3   Lansbury, *My Life*, p. 19.

4   Ibid., p. 23.

5   Postgate, *Life of George Lansbury*, p. 8.

6   S. Mayor, *The Churches and the Labour Movement*, Independent Press, 1967, p. 22.

7   Ibid., p. 21.

8   Lansbury, *My Life*, pp. 37–38.

9   Ibid., p. 37.

10   Ibid., p. 45.

11   Ibid., p. 51.

12   Ibid., p. 53.

2

INTO POLITICS

On returning to Britain, the Lansburys dwelt in a succession of different homes, nearly all in the East End of London. It was the East End of Tower Hamlets (including the districts of Bow and Poplar which Lansbury was to frequent) where Charles Booth discovered 35 per cent of the population living at or below his poverty line of twenty-one shillings per week for a family. It was the East End of the wretchedly-treated match girls whom Annie Besant stimulated to strike against Bryant and Mays. It was the East End which drew Dr Barnardo and General Booth. It was the East End of Jack the Ripper. It was the East End where poverty, overcrowding and lack of sanitation led, in some districts, to annual death rates of 25 per 1000 persons and a death rate for children aged one and under of 227 per 1000 births. Yet, as the historian Fishman points out, in his graphic and penetrating analysis of this period, despite all the distress, many inhabitants did have jobs, did pay the rent and did want to improve the area.[1] Lansbury was such a person.

So Lansbury had found a location. He also had a job at thirty shillings a week in his father-in-law's wood yard. The Mr Brine whom Lansbury once depicted as a bully showed him much kindness and not only gave him a job but also allowed him time off to pursue a campaign against the false promises of emigration societies. A handbill, in the Lansbury Collection in the London School of Economics' archives, announces a committee including a Mr G. Lansbury and a Mr W. Sewell. The committee organized a conference in February 1886, at which officials from the emigration societies anticipated easily putting down Lansbury the workman. Instead, he delivered a well-prepared speech backed by figures showing the fate of people lured abroad by emigration propaganda. It swung the conference to his side and led to a deputation which successfully prevailed upon the government to establish its

Emigration Information Department.

Present at the conference was an influential Liberal MP, Samuel Montagu. He identified young Lansbury as the kind of man who could win working-class votes for his party and approached him saying, '. . . you must let us get you into the House of Commons.'[2] Whether Lansbury's ambition to become an MP originated at this point is not known. What is clear is that at the 1886 general election, Lansbury acted as agent for Montagu, who was one of the few Liberals to increase his majority. He then became the unpaid secretary of the Bow and Bromley Liberal Association, which selected J.A. Murray MacDonald as its parliamentary candidate with a radical programme of manhood suffrage, free education and an eight-hour working day.

In parliamentary terms, British politics was dominated by two parties, the Conservatives and the Liberals. Like a number of working men, Lansbury regarded the latter as his party but he now discovered that not many of its members shared the radical views of Murray MacDonald. Indeed, a large number believed in a virtually unfettered free market with any state intervention kept to a minimum and so were opposed to legislation for an eight-hour working day. Lansbury had taken up this issue and, in one meeting, cleverly pointed out that the Liberals were urging the government to alleviate distress in Ireland by fixing rents, that is by intervening in the free market. He attended the conference of the National Liberal Federation in 1889 determined to press the matter despite the pleas of prominent Liberals that it was too contentious. When he mounted the platform to move his resolution, pandemonium broke out and he was pushed off. Lansbury wrote that 'thus ended my connection with Liberalism[3].

The eight-hour dispute was the occasion, not the cause, of the break. Lansbury had perceived that Liberal policies might alleviate but would not substantially alter the lot of working people. Simultaneously, he was learning about and being attracted to socialism from three sources.

First, he came into contact with the Socialist Democratic Federation (SDF) whose members argued that no real change would occur in society until working-class people controlled their own destinies, namely by having a party distinct from both Conservatives and Liberals. This made sense, for at the time — as Lansbury later told in an article in the *Labour Leader* in 1912 — he was perceiving that rents paid by working-class tenants went less on improving their property and more on paying for 'the great City banquets'. Lansbury now wanted a system whereby the tenants decided how the rents were spent. Much of the socialist propaganda fitted in with Lansbury's belief in a Christianity which pulled down the oppressors and lifted up the oppressed.

He was also impressed by the lives and arguments of certain individuals, all of whom became his friends. These were Will Crooks, Ben Tillett, Will Thorn and Charlie Sumner. They were working class, upright, honest and mainly socialist. Lansbury was drawn to them and their socialism.

Lansbury had also come to recognize the importance of trade unions. Tillett was one of the organizers of the famous dock strike of 1889 and Lansbury threw in his support. Here he witnessed both the effectiveness of working-class leadership and the loyalty and solidarity of the often-despised dockers. In the same year, Lansbury joined what became the National Union of Municipal and General Workers. He wrote years later, 'I was a general labourer earning 30s a week when I joined the union and I have remained a general worker ever since.'[4] He remained a union member for the rest of his life. Lansbury humorously pointed out that the first strike was by the children of Israel when they refused to make bricks and he went on to argue that strikes were a legitimate weapon for workers to use against the powerful. He perceived that trade unions would play an increasing part in the socialist movement, a movement which would have to be in the hands of working-class people.

Lansbury's openness about his growing allegiance to socialism alarmed his Liberal colleagues. They made strenuous efforts to stop him leaving. Finally, Montagu called him to a meeting at the Commons. Lansbury explained what happened:

'I told him I had become a Socialist and wanted to preach socialism. He replied: 'Don't be silly, I am a Socialist, a better Socialist than you. I give a tenth of my riches each year to the poor.' I said: 'Yes, I know how good you are and respect you more than it is possible to say, but, my dear friend, we Socialists want to prevent you getting the nine-tenths. We do not believe in rich and poor and charity. We want to create wealth and all the means of life and share them equally among the people.'[5]

Montagu, an immensely rich man, went on to offer Lansbury five pounds a week until he obtained a safe parliamentary seat. He refused the tempting offer but then proceeded to fulfil a promise to act as Liberal agent for Murray MacDonald in the election of 1892. The night after, he and a few friends left to form the Bow and Bromley branch of the SDF.

The courage of Lansbury's decision is not easy to appreciate today. The Liberals were offering him financial security and, as Lansbury recorded, 'I was a poor man, struggling with poverty, and the temptation to stay where I was with the Liberals was very strong indeed.'[6] If elected as a socialist, he would receive no income, for MPs were not paid by the state. However, the chances of being elected were slim. Voting rights were held by only a minority of the population. The Labour Party was not even in existence. But principle was all to Lansbury and perhaps that is why he preserved a letter from the radical Liberal MP, Henry Watkinson, who wrote:

I rejoice that you had the courage to stand true to your convictions . . . I would rather know you as a poor and obscure friend than as the many men whom I see around who 'did run well'.

The socialism to which Lansbury committed himself had no single entity. Geoffrey Foote, in his history of the Labour Party's political evolution, states, 'It was in the turmoil of the 1880s that the different and conflicting views which were to make up the ideas of British socialism were formed and fought over.'[7] Among these conflicting and different forces, four were particularly important and Lansbury had some links with all of them.

The most intellectual body was the Fabian Society formed in 1884. In general, it stood for reform of existing institutions rather than wholesale change and for gradual improvements via the ballot-box rather than by revolution. With members such as Shaw, the Webbs and Wells, the Fabian Society had considerable public influence. Lansbury, however, had little enthusiasm for the Fabians and later, in the *Labour Leader* of 1912, wrote, 'I always had the feeling . . . that Fabians were much too clever and superior for ordinary persons like myself to be associated with.' Nonetheless, he did admire Annie Besant, a Fabian at that time, and he did read the Fabian publications.

The most working-class bodies were the trade unions. At this time, many trade unionists supported the Liberals and some of their officials became MPs (known as Lib-Labs). But an increasing number — such as Will Thorn and Ben Tillett — were arguing that they needed representation quite separate from parties which were dominated by the employers. Lansbury agreed, and Postgate wrote that with them he 'felt a complete understanding, an almost physical sense of unity that he had with every man or woman of working-class origin who was treading the same political path that he was'.[8]

The most radical body was the SDF, which stood for a wholesale restructuring of society achieved, if necessary, by a violent working-class revolution. Oddly enough, its leader was no son of the soil or factory floor. Instead it was the charismatic Henry Hyndman, a wealthy gentleman, educated at Cambridge, and a distinguished amateur cricketer.

Despite his upper-class background, Hyndman adopted Marxist ideas and in 1881 founded the SDF as a socialist body intent on the overthrow of capitalism. Hyndman inspired Lansbury to read Marx and persuaded many other working-class people that they should aim for an economic system which they controlled and a political one which got rid of people like himself.

The Fabian Society, the trade unions and the SDF were prominent organizations which advanced socialism. In addition, socialist thought and practice were developed by a number of outstanding individuals whom Geoffrey Foote calls the Ethical Socialists. For instance, he points to Robert Blatchford, the author of *Merrie England*, and John Bruce and Katherine Glasier whose books were read by Lansbury. Such writers emphasized the socially immoral state of a society which tolerated widespread social deprivations in the midst of enormous wealth and they looked forward to a new society based on co-operative principles. Foote also classes Keir Hardie and Ramsay MacDonald in this group, for they took a strong ethical stance, much of which was drawn from the New Testament. But they were also practical organizers and it was Hardie who inspired the formation of the Scottish Labour Party in 1888 and MacDonald who became a leading member of the Independent Labour Party soon after its establishment in 1893.

Lansbury was to be associated with all these streams of socialism, but his initial formal links were with the SDF, for whom he became an unpaid organizer and traveller. He had declared to Montagu his desire to become a socialist preacher and so almost every Saturday, after finishing work, he would leave London for the provinces, do a meeting on Saturday night, three on Sunday, and catch the night train back, ready to start work at seven o'clock on Monday morning.[9]

He covered the length and breadth of Britain and everywhere he carried a red flag which, if the train passed near his house, he would wave through the carriage window at his children. Frequently he had to walk home from King's Cross Station, for he lacked any money for the fare to the East End.

In Glasgow, in Birmingham or in the open air at his local Victoria Park, Lansbury's message was the same, that only socialism could abolish poverty, unemployment and injustice. His concern and vision were not restricted to Britain. He welcomed socialist refugees from other countries, and Christopher Hill, in his biography of Lenin, reveals that in 1907 when Lenin came to London for a congress, 'George Lansbury helped him to obtain a substantial loan from Mr Fels, a wealthy manufacturer'.[10] Further, in an age of imperialism, Lansbury was unusual in his insistence that socialism should involve equality for all races. In a speech, reported in *The Arbitrator* of May 1892, he exhorted:

> Let us refuse (either as individuals or as a nation) to sanction
> the increase of wealth at the expense of others, be they white,
> yellow, red or black men. Let us remember that the mere
> accident of being born in a special part of the globe should
> not confer any special privilege or power upon anyone. Let us
> refuse to claim for ourselves any right we will not recognize as
> due to others.

Such sentiments provoked much hostility. At an open-air meeting in Burnley, a factory hooter was set off to drown him but his stentorian voice triumphed. At Oxford in 1892, his way to the platform was barred by a mob of students. A socialist colleague, whose job was to sweep the students' chimneys, promptly asked his daughters to lead the platform party and the young 'gentlemen' felt obliged to stand aside. Other meetings were marred by rowdiness and violence.

The Lansbury Collection contains a number of letters which show that Lansbury's efforts were much appreciated. His readiness to travel long distances, his refusal to accept any fees, his politeness combined with a refusal to compromise, were making him well known in socialist circles. More important, his abilities as a speaker were helping to communicate socialism. Not only was there no television or radio but also there was no national daily paper with socialist views. Fabians might write books but few could afford them. The spread of socialism thus depended heavily upon its evangelists who week in and week out spoke at public meetings. Of these preachers, Lansbury's talent for holding working-class audiences made his contribution to the winning of people to socialism as important as that of the great socialist figure, Keir Hardie.

Lansbury's role as a socialist preacher is all the more remarkable if it is considered that, in addition, he was working long hours at a manual job, was contesting various elections, and was helping his wife cope with an ever-increasing family. And, as his reputation grew, so his home became a calling point for many seeking advice about legal, financial and personal difficulties. Postgate comments: 'The advice was almost invariably good and well-informed, and quite invariably kind. The assistance was limited by his own strained circumstances.'[11] Despite these pressures, Lansbury continued to devote himself to socialism. One reason he did so was his burning anger at the blight of unemployment.

The trade union organizer, Margaret Bondfield, writes of this time that unemployment was accepted as a fact of life: 'The periodical wagelessness of masses of men . . . was either ignored or, when recognized as an evil, was regarded as unavoidable.'[12] Lansbury was not prepared to ignore it. All his life, he had observed the results of unemployment, and now he was living in the borough of Poplar which, as the historian Ryan points out, was among the most deprived in London.[13] He witnessed the casual dockers system where men presented themselves for work and the unlucky ones were sent away with nothing. He saw times of recession swell the numbers of those out of jobs who were then forced to apply to the Poor Law. He lived in an area where hungry men and women broke into the Poplar bakery to find bread. In the snowy January of 1894, he was at the receiving end when his home was besieged by between four- and five-hundred men demanding work but, as a Poor Law Guardian, he possessed no powers to help them. Lansbury believed that in the long term only a socialist system would remove unemployment. In the short term, he was prepared to agitate and campaign in order to modify it.

Faced with an unemployment level of 12 per cent, the Conservative government did allow the passing of the 1905 Unemployed Workman's Act which permitted local Distress Committees to organize public work for the unemployed. In reality its provisions were slight, for public money was sanctioned only for the organization of schemes and not for the wages of those who worked them. Nowhere was the disappointment more bitter than in Poplar where, in the three months preceding October, the Board of Guardians received fresh applications covering 10,589 persons. The Poplar Borough Council petitioned King Edward to no avail. Lansbury then persuaded the prime minister, A.J. Balfour, to receive a deputation. On the appointed day, some 6,000 women marched on the offices of the Local Government Board. Lansbury wrote:

> We did not have a single middle-class organiser to help us locally — in fact, these women and girls needed no organising, they just organised themselves.[14]

A deputation went into Balfour with Lansbury pointing out the limitations of the act and several women depicting the plight of their families. Balfour offered sympathy but little else and was content to argue that it was not the role of government to interfere in the workings of the economy.

The demonstration did receive enormous press coverage. *The Times* gave it five full columns while the *Evening Times* reported, 'It was plain that many of the women were actually starving.' An unexpected outcome was that Queen Alexandra made an appeal which led to public donations of £150,000 to the Distress Committees. The demonstration had won something.

Lansbury participated in other demonstrations. He also pursued the issue in public meetings. In addressing the Christian Social Union in May 1907, he explained that unemployment was created not by loafers but because 'industry is so organised that there is always a margin of workers for whom . . . no work can be found'. The answer, therefore, was not royal charity to boost Distress Committees but government action to alter the way in which industry was run. And, for his part, Lansbury was giving more and more of his time to securing socialist representation in local and central government.

An SDF handbill in the Lansbury Collection shows George

Lansbury, veneer drier, as a candidate for Poor Law Guardian. He was successful in 1892 and the following chapter will concentrate on his achievements within the Poor Law. In November 1903, he won a place on the Poplar Metropolitan Borough Council. Immediately, he strove to increase the wages of council employees and he retained a letter of 8 September 1904 from a roadman, Mr Collins, who wrote that 'it has made our circumstances (which were none too easy on 25/6d a week) very much more comfortable, the addition of 4/6d weekly being indeed a great boon to us'. In 1910, Lansbury was elected to the London County Council where he served for three years.

Lansbury was to remain a Guardian and local authority councillor for much of his life. But his sights were also on Westminster. During the 1890s, he twice stood as parliamentary candidate for the SDF at Walworth. He secured few votes yet had an experience which strengthened his resolve. He was leaving the count, dejected with his 340 votes:

> All of a sudden an old Irish woman with tears in her eyes and voice, flung her arms around me, smothered me with kisses and said . . . 'Never mind: you are bound to win. Don't you ever despair' . . . I was choked and crying like a child because in a flash I realised that people like this poor woman were beginning to trust me.[15]

Encouraged, Lansbury stood again at Bow and Bromley in 1900 with a manifesto calling for votes for all adults, the nationalization of land and railways, work for the unemployed and funds for the elderly. By now he was parting company with the SDF. A major reason was that Lansbury, as a pacifist, was unhappy with Hyndman's insistence on the necessity for a violent revolution. So, some time about 1903, Lansbury began to stand under the name of the Labour Representation Committee. The LRC was an attempt to bring together socialist bodies in order to put forward at elections Labour candidates who were independent of other parties. With Ramsay MacDonald as secretary, it raised sufficient funds to contribute to MPs' expenses. In the 1906 election, Lansbury stood at Middlesborough where he finished bottom of the poll.

The 1906 general election resulted in a landslide Liberal victory. Nontheless, the LRC had fielded fifty candidates, nearly all working-class men, and won twenty-nine seats with victories for Ramsay MacDonald, Keir Hardie, Philip Snowden and Arthur Henderson. MacDonald's recent biographer says that 'this general election saw the parliamentary breakthrough of the LRC'.[16] But the name LRC faded away as the small band of MPs decided to call themselves the Labour Party.

Despite his defeat, Lansbury's reputation as a candidate was even more firmly established. In November 1907, he addressed meetings in Scotland, and a newspaper cutting, preserved by Lansbury, reported what he said at Paisley:

> The whole of Britain is improperly arranged: the idea of the socialist is not pulling down but building up: we want men and women all over the world to join hands together until we have built a new society, a new order which will bring the best means for a new life (loud and prolonged applause).

Lansbury had attracted large audiences in Scotland and one result was an invitation to stand as parliamentary candidate for Paisley. However, his heart was now set on Bow, where he lived at 103 St Stephen's Road, and in the January 1910 election he stood as candidate for Bow and Bromley. He finished second and might well have won except for the intervention of John Clifford, a famous Nonconformist minister and passionate opponent of denominational education, who was convinced that Lansbury supported the teaching of the Anglican faith in state schools. There soon followed another election, in December 1910, and this time Lansbury was successful. Thus democratic elections took him into the three spheres which occupied so much of his life: the Poor Law, local and central government.

The 1910 election involved Lansbury in some religious controversy. His faith had to develop during these years alongside his other views. For a time, approximately 1890–1900, he stopped attending church and removed his children from the Christian Sunday school. He wrote that 'for a period when I left the Church . . . they attended the Ethical Sunday School in Bow organized and conducted by the prince of teachers, F.J. Gould'.[17] Gould was a militant atheist. Lansbury's withdrawal from the church was noted sadly in a letter to him from the Rev. Kitto in 1893. It appears that Lansbury became disillusioned with many clergymen who tolerated poverty, condemned strikes and took no action to relieve unemployment. Some even attacked his proposals for spending public money on the poor.

However, not all Anglican clergy were of this ilk. Churchmen such as bishops Randall Thomas Davidson and Charles Gore were sympathetic towards socialism, and the latter became president of the Christian Social Union which was founded in 1893 to consider how Christianity could be applied to social problems. Further, for all his disillusionment with some Christians, Lansbury did not completely lose his faith in Christ. By 1900, he was approaching the church again and then an important part was played by Cosmo Lang, Bishop of Stepney from 1901 to 1908. He recorded:

> One Sunday afternoon I came to preach at Bow Church. The Rector, Manley Power, . . . sent me word that a very interesting man with whom he had been having some talks might be there and would meet me at supper afterwards. He was a secularist lecturer, by name Lansbury, who seemed to be feeling his way back to the Church. He came to Bow Church, very shamefacedly, and sat in the back behind a pillar. After supper, he poured out doubts, questions, desires, as out of a long-corked-up bottle; and I was much moved by his sincerity. Thereafter, he threw in his lot with the Church, taking St Francis of Assisi as his ideal Christian . . . Shortly after our talk at Bow Rectory, I asked him if he would give his witness to the Christian faith at a big men's meeting to be held at Bow Baths. He said it would not be easy, but he would do his best. It was advertised that he would speak. There was a great crowd — hundreds of the kind of collarless men not usually seen at such meetings. They listened quietly to me but when Lansbury rose there was an outcry — shouts of 'Traitor!', 'Judas!', and so forth. I shall never forget the way in which Lansbury turned on them — 'Is this the freedom of speech you claim for yourselves?' etc. — and gave his witness and impelled silence.[18]

Much helped by a friendship with a curate, the Rev. William Corbett Roberts, Lansbury then threw himself enthusiastically into church life. Not only did he become a regular communicant, he also started a Bible class for boys where he answered 'with sincerity and the wisdom of experience the sceptical questions of the young, primed to the muzzle with the atheistic teachings of Robert Blatchford'.[19] When time allowed, he even supported the church football team at Hackney Marshes, where his loud voice urged on his son Edgar and team mates.

Edgar recorded that the children 'were all amazed at the turn of events'.[20] Nonetheless, they followed his lead and Edgar enjoyed the walks to church where '... we would discuss the many thorns and stumbling blocks in the path of the believer'.[21] Lansbury's involvement in church Sunday activities meant that he now spent more time with his family and Edgar considered that his father's 'happiest days were those which followed his return to the fold of the church'.[22]

From childhood, Lansbury had hated the injustices and sufferings he saw all around. As he grew into manhood, he accepted socialism both as a means of critically investigating society and as a means of change. Yet it should be appreciated that much of his socialism stemmed from his understanding of Christianity. In his many writings and speeches, he frequently referred to the Bible but rarely to Marx. Thus he wrote:

> I am a socialist pure and simple . . . I have come to believe that the motive power which should and which *will*, if men allow it, work our social salvation, is the power which comes from a belief in Christ and His message to man.'[23]

After his return to the church, Lansbury made no secret of the links between his socialism and his Christianity.

When the Church Socialist League was formed in 1906, Lansbury joined and became its vice-president. The League was the first Anglican society committed to socialism. Its four principles were to 'cultivate the life of brotherhood by the use of prayer and sacrament', 'give practical effect to the sex equality proclaimed by the sacraments of the Church' 'help the advance of socialism'; and 'convert Church peoples to the principles of socialism.' Later, Lansbury accepted the position of president and, in 1912, led a League demonstration of 500 marchers, with a cross at the head, to Lambeth Palace to protest at the church hierarchy's failure to help the unemployed.

In his speeches and writings, Lansbury continued to attack some church leaders both for accepting the capitalist god of profit and for neglecting the poor. In 1906, in a chapter of a book which discussed why working-class people were alienated from the church, he condemned the views of many clergy as 'the wretched abortion passed off as Christianity' and continued:

> Let them not only voice the wrongs of the people, but let
> them denounce the commercial life which pays people to tell
> lies, which adulterates and cheats, which sweats the poor and
> exploits the workers . . . Let them preach the equal value
> not only of our souls but of our bodies also. Let them teach
> that the rich are rich because the poor are poor. Then, I
> am sure, even the common people would gladly throng our
> churches.[24]

Through the League's meetings, his publications and his speeches, Lansbury became publicly identified as a socialist and Christian. With less publicity, he helped young Christians who approached him because they were puzzled at the hostility of many church leaders to state reforms designed to alleviate poverty. Thus, in September 1907, he received a letter from Septimus Dawson, possibly a former Sunday school pupil, who complained that his Baptist minister preached that socialism pampered the working classes. Eventually, George spoke at his church. Other letters in the Lansbury Collection are from clergymen who appreciated that he expressed their interpretation of the gospel. And it was not just the lowly curates who wrote. In 1908, Cosmo Lang, as he left to become Archbishop of York, sent a considerable sum of money saying that George Lansbury could use it more effectively than the church and adding, in a handwritten note:

> I have always looked upon you as a comrade in my work . . . I
> don't want to lose the link you have between the Church and
> Labour. But anyway I shall often think of the first time when
> I met you and pray that God may use you for His Kingdom of
> the Christ and the good of the people.

Socialist organizer, Guardian, councillor, writer, churchman — in the midst of all these roles it is easy to forget that Lansbury had a personal life. Yet, with a large family, he could hardly avoid a full and busy one. Bessie and George had their share of troubles in these years with three of their children dying: young George, after surviving various illnesses in Australia, in 1889; Doreen (the twin of Constance) in 1902; and their eldest and married daughter, Bessie Haverson, in 1909.

Death and poverty were commonplace for many Victorians. The Lansburys suffered both. At least George had a regular job, but his wage was low and there were many mouths to feed. Edgar recalled that they 'were always hard put to it to scrape together lump sums for rates, rent, coal bills, and small but regular school fees'.[25] The most common meal, he continued, was bread and cheese and often it lacked the cheese. So hard up were George and Bessie that in 1892 they had to borrow fifty shillings from Wait and Alice Sewell which they repaid at two bob a week.

Amazingly, for all their limited resources, George was continually helping others. His brother Jim was unemployed in 1894 and 1895 and, following desperate hand-delivered notes, George gave him money. His generosity was not confined to relatives, for the needy were always knocking at his door. Edgar amusingly tells of one occasion when his father went so far as to take out a loan to help a friend start a business. Bessie was furious for they were short themselves yet, as Edgar continued, 'the money was repaid, mother's guns were spiked, and father provided with a powerful text on the integrity of borrowers and the goodness of men in general.'[26]

About 1896 Mr Brine died and George took over as a partner in the saw mill and timber firm. He possessed considerable business acumen for — despite his many other commitments — it prospered. George got on particularly well with Jewish immigrants from Poland and Russia who were settling in the East End and who purchased wood for their trades. The friendships between the socialist Christian and the Jewish craftsmen were to endure. The latter devoted much of their lives to their occupations whereas for George Lansbury it was different. He disliked intensely the capitalist god of profit and regarded the timber firm as a means of producing a useful commodity while supporting himself and others. Edgar remembered:

The curate recommended a pimply-faced, anaemic-looking youth; a fellow guardian urged the claims of a consumptive old fellow with only a few months to live . . . all would be taken on whatever their qualifications for the actual work.[27]

The partnership did mean financial security and from henceforth the Lansburys did not have to endure the material hardships of their early years. In particular, it eased the lot of Bessie Lansbury. It is tempting to regard Bessie only as the wife of George and the mother of their children. The suffragette leader Sylvia Pankhurst said of her:

> Her exceptionally large family had long debarred her from activity in the Labour Movement; her part had been the harder one of lonely sacrifice and harsh economy.[28]

Yet this is not the whole truth.

As will be shown in a subsequent chapter, Bessie had doubts about the middle-class leadership of the suffragette movement and was not always enthusiastic in backing people like Sylvia. But she often did participate as an activist in local groups. For a while, in the early years of marriage, she led a girls' club and she remained a supporter of a number of local causes. She attended classes on Marx and Engels and, later in life, after she and George visited Russia, she became a much firmer admirer of Russian communism than he did. During the First World War, Bessie was involved in groups which attempted to alleviate the plight of soldiers' families. Indeed, for a while, she was the director of The Mothers' Arms, a centre which looked after children for mothers. Moreover, she later identified with Sylvia Pankhurst's Women's Suffrage Federation but only after it broadened out into a socialist movement rather than one which focused just on votes for women. In short, Bessie was not content just to stay at home and be a pale reflection of her husband. She had a mind and activities of her own.

For all her political interests, Bessie's life did revolve mainly around the home. In all, she bore twelve children: Bessie, Annie, George, William, Edgar, Dorothy, Daisy, Nellie, Doreen and Constance, Violet and Eric. The deaths of three of the children and their initial low income brought both sorrows and hardships. As in most families there were times of anxiety, as when William, aged fifteen, ran away to sea and when Edgar got sacked from his first job. Yet Edgar describes a happy home. Bessie ensured that all the children had their tasks to do and combined firmness with affection. George was a benign father who helped in the washing and changing of the children, who loved playing with them and who organized regular trips to the park. The children never appeared to resent the time their parents gave to politics and, interestingly, nearly all became socialists themselves.

The Lansburys had to make their own entertainments. Bessie played a small, portable organ while the children struggled with violins, mouth organs and cornets. George led their singsongs in a baritone voice, with a repertoire of comic ditties, socialist songs, love pieces and hymns. They joined the local socialist band which was noted more for its enthusiasm than its ability. At one gathering, Edgar recalled, it refused to stop playing 'The Caliph of Bagdad' even when the speaker was ready:

At last the chairman resorted to force, slammed the keyboard cover on the hands of the player, while others forcibly restrained the fiddlers . . . On these occasions it must have been difficult for the speaker to put over the socialist message of brotherhood and of peace. I know father didn't try, he just roared with laughter.[29]

Bessie and George enjoyed a satisfying marriage. She did regret that he was away so much and they did have some arguments. But Edgar reveals that Bessie never grumbled about those absences, while any differences were soon made up with 'a dozen, twenty, or even fifty kisses, with the whole family gaping at them (where could we go? — there was only one living room and that was the kitchen)'.[30] For his part, George:

never returned after more than a day's absence without bringing her flowers, not orchids or lilies, but a penny bunch of violets, a sprig of heather, or maybe some lilies of the valley or forget-me-nots.[31]

And always, no matter how late he returned from socialist meetings, Bessie was waiting up for him. George and Bessie Lansbury were united in all aspects of their life. But George insisted that:

the thanks are due to her and no one else, because she has borne the loneliness of life without any regret, feeling sure the work we were trying to do was for the good of mankind.[32]

References

1   W. Fishman, *East End 1888*, Duckworth, 1988, Chapter 3.

2   G. Lansbury, *My Life*, Constable, 1928, p. 63.

3   Ibid., p. 73.

4   G. Lansbury, *Looking Backwards and Forwards*, Blackie & Son, 1935, p. 53.

5   Lansbury, *My Life*, p. 75.

6   Ibid., p. 73.

7   G. Foote, *The Labour Party's Political Thought: A History*, Croom Helm, 1985, p. 19.

8   R. Postgate, *The Life of George Lansbury*, Longmans, Green & Co., 1951, pp. 32–33.

9   Lansbury, *My Life*, p. 76.

10 C. Hill, *Lenin and the Russian Revolution*, 4th impression, English Universities Press, 1957, p. 40.

11 Postgate, *Life of George Lansbury*, p. 104.

12 M. Bondfield, *A Life's Work*, Hutchinson and Co., 1948, pp. 263–64.

13 P. Ryan, 'Poplarism 1894–1930', in P. Thane (ed.), *The Origins of British Social Policy*, Croom Helm, 1978, p. 57.

14 Lansbury, *Looking Backwards*, p. 102.

15 Ibid., p. 87.

16 A. Morgan, *J. Ramsay MacDonald*, Manchester University Press, 1987, p. 39.

17 Lansbury, *My Life*, p. 77.

18 Cited in J.G. Lockhart, *Cosmo Gordon Lang*, Hodder and Stoughton, 1949, pp. 160–61.

19 E. Lansbury, *George Lansbury, My Father*, Sampson Low, Marston & Co., 193, p. 118.

20 Ibid., p. 119.

21 Ibid., p. 120.

22 Ibid., p. 117.

23 Cited in Postgate, *Life of George Lansbury*, p. 56.

24 'G. Lansbury', chapter in G. Haw (ed.), *Christianity and the Working Classes*, Macmillan and Co., 1906, pp. 180, 178–79.

25 E. Lansbury, *George Lansbury*, p. 65.

26 Ibid., pp. 65–66.

27 Ibid., p. 123.

28 S. Pankhurst, *The Suffragette Movement*, Virago, 1978, pp. 426–27.

29 E. Lansbury, *George Lansbury*, p. 113.

30 Ibid., p. 88.

31 Ibid., p. 143.

32 Lansbury, *My Life*, p. 76.

3

THE GUARDIAN

During the 1890s, people without income could apply to the Poor Law. Its origins went back at least to the Elizabethan Relief Act of 1601 but its administrative practices and principles had been set down by the Poor Law Amendment Act of 1834. After 1871, the Local Government Board was the central government body responsible for overseeing the Poor Law nationally, while locally parishes (or unions of parishes) elected Boards of Guardians to appoint and supervise the main officials, particularly the relieving officer who controlled applications for help and the master who ran the workhouse. Funds came from a local rate levied on householders.

Applicants could not be received into the workhouse until they had sold all but their most essential goods. Once admitted they were subjected to a harsh regime where uniforms were worn, men separated from women, and where all were expected to work at tasks like scrubbing floors, breaking stones and picking oakum. The 1834 act required that their lot be worse than that of the lowest labourer outside. At least they were fed and the Poor Law historian, M. A. Crowther, explains that their lot was worse less in terms of loss of food and more in terms of loss of personal freedom.[1]

Not all workhouses were ruled by cruel masters of the kind portrayed by Charles Dickens. They were not all run on identical lines. For instance, differences occurred as to whether children, the sick and the mentally ill were separated from other inmates. Further, not all provision was based on the workhouse, and out-relief could be given in their own homes to what were considered deserving cases.

Despite these differences, the Poor Law had three undoubted and damaging features. Primarily, it conveyed to inmates — or potential inmates — a sense of dread, stigma and personal failure. Indeed, as Nigel Middleton demonstrates, many people died of starvation rather than enter the workhouse doors, while hundreds of parentless children preferred to live on the streets.[2] Lansbury reflected this fear in his account of his first visit to the Poplar workhouse. He wrote of:

> hard forms, whitewashed walls, keys dangling at the waist of those who spoke to you, huge books for name, history, etc., searching, and then being stripped and bathed in a communal tub . . . everything possible was done to inflict mental and moral degradation.[3]

Another drawback was that the Poor Law broke up families. By keeping parents and children apart, the workhouse lessened the regular contact so essential to family unity. By insisting that those entering its portals had parted with their material possessions, the system made it more difficult for parents ever to discharge themselves to create new homes. Lansbury, who placed enormous value on family life, soon perceived that the Victorian Britain which exalted the virtues of the family was really concerned with middle-class families while allowing the families of the poor to go to the wall.

Furthermore, the Poor Law did not equip its children for the future. They were directed into domestic service, farm labouring and the armed forces. Yet these were the very occupations listed by most adults applying to the Poor Law, for they were associated with low wages, frequent dismissals and little opportunity for saving. Again, Lansbury soon identified the failings in the education and preparation of children at Poor Law schools.

Outside the Poor Law, some did seek relief from the growing number of Victorian charities. Lansbury was always a supporter of local charitable effort but he had mixed feelings about some of the larger, more powerful societies. The Salvation Army was established in the East End at this time and Lansbury — who heard William and Catherine Booth preach at Mile End Waste even before their Salvation Army days — observed them closely. Initially he was critical of their narrow theology and, as a fiery socialist, considered Mrs Booth's social work as a kind of bandage on a corrupt social system. Later he admitted that 'we were hopelessly wrong and she was right . . . The victims of the system were broken and injured all around us, and the "ambulance work" of Mrs Booth was absolutely necessary'.[4] In particular, he admired Catherine's compassion towards and lack of condemnation of unmarried mothers. Further, Fishman identifies features of William Booth which must have appealed to Lansbury. He preached that the poor wanted work not charity; he believed in state services to modify the distress caused by capitalism; and he was sympathetic towards socialism.[5] Lansbury would have disliked the undemocratic nature of the Salvation Army hierarchy but he always praised the devotion of its officers, and the Lansbury Collection contains several letters from them which reveal their mutual regard.

The Salvation Army provided relief within the East End. Dr Barnardo eventually decided it was best to remove the most needy children from that environment. His compassionate heart had been moved by the plight of children who lived on the streets. He understood why they shunned what he called the 'huge barrack workhouses, where all the inmates lost their rights and individuality'.[6] In response, he formed his own children's homes. Barnardo's first lodgings in the East End were near to Lansbury's home and it is curious that the Lansbury Collection contains no reference to him. Barnardo was opposed both to socialism and the state provision of extensive social services, but these factors would not have dimmed Lansbury's appreciation of Barnardo's love for children. What may well have annoyed him was Barnardo's attitude towards the parents of the children — for he declared, 'I take from a very low class,' — and his reluctance to return children to such parents.[7] By contrast, Lansbury had a deep sympathy for and understanding of parents who found it difficult to cope and he was always saddened by the separation of children from parents, no matter how poor and deprived they were.

It was this class factor which also shaped Lansbury's attitude towards another famous philanthropic institution, Toynbee Hall. Toynbee Hall was a Settlement which served as a base for ex-public-school and Oxbridge men to spend some time working among the poor. Lansbury appreciated some of the educational classes and clubs organized by Toynbee Hall, and Pimlott, in his history of Toynbee Hall, points out that he gave a number of talks there on subjects such as St Francis of Assisi.[8] Nonetheless, Lansbury was convinced that Toynbee Hall perpetuated rather than lessened class differences. He was not against middle-class people living in the East End and he spoke warmly of the radical priest, Stuart Headlam, and his 'splendid years of service on behalf of our London children', for Headlam had resided in an ordinary house in the area.[9] By contrast, he pointed out that the experience of the Toynbee young men 'only extended to meetings . . . in Toynbee Hall and its fine parlour, dining and other rooms'.[10] In his view, they never really belonged to the East End.

Lansbury's antagonism towards Toynbee Hall was also linked with its close association with the Charity Organisation Society (COS). The Settlement served as the headquarters of the local branch of the COS, which received strong support from Toynbee's warden, the Rev. Samuel Barnett. The COS had been formed in 1869 in order to co-ordinate charities and to avoid duplication among them. Under Charles Loch it became of national importance and strongly influenced both the course of voluntary agencies and the development of social work. The COS advocated and practised the strictest scrutiny of every applicant for help and divided the poor into the 'deserving' who merited charitable relief and the 'undeserving' who should be directed to the Poor Law.

In Lansbury's younger days, his mother had fed some poor families. The local COS actually asked her not to succour them and, when George complained, Barnett replied that 'the workhouse was the best place for such people'. Lansbury continued in his account of the incident: 'This message and my later inquiries made me a most bitter enemy of the Charity Organization Society and all its works.'[11] To be fair, Barnett later parted company with the COS, but its pattern of using affluent, middle-class outsiders to judge the merits of poor and often starving people remained and Lansbury was always ferocious in his criticisms of it.

The COS, being a powerful body, obtained the election of some of its members as Poor Law Guardians. As Guardians, they advocated denying all out-door relief to the able-bodied and offered the workhouse even to widows and the elderly. Lansbury decided to stand for election himself. The historian Crowther makes a special note of him, describing him as 'a man of extraordinary kindness and generosity', for it was unusual to have a working-class candidate.[12] But stand he did and in 1892, at the age of thirty-three, he won a place as a Guardian for the Poplar Union which covered the parishes of Bow, Bromley St Leonard's and Poplar.

Lansbury disliked the patronizing nature of middle-class voluntary bodies. He hated the Poor Law. He always advocated its abolition and in 1911 he was to publish a pamphlet entitled

Smash the Workhouse. However, until that day he was determined to improve it. His attitude could hardly have been more different from that of other Guardians, the gentlefolk from the COS, the local businessmen and the private landlords whose main concerns were to deter so-called malingerers and to keep down costs. As if to distance himself from them, Lansbury arrived at his first meeting collarless and sprinkled with sawdust from the wood mill he had just left. He refused a cup of tea unless he could pay for it. His action might now seem petty, but he was wanting to show himself different from those Guardians who took large meals and attended conferences at public expense while begrudging the slightest luxury to workhouse inmates.

Lansbury was not alone. Also elected was Will Crooks, a Poplar man who himself had spent part of his boyhood in the workhouse. Like Lansbury, he was a trade unionist, a Christian, and later a councillor and MP. He now took a seat in the very room where, as a frightened child, he had been received into the institution thirty years before. The election of Crooks and Lansbury had been possible because the property qualification for the post of Guardian had been lowered. Soon it was abolished altogether and they were joined by three other working-class Guardians. They remained a minority for some years but by dint of acting together and marshalling their arguments they became the driving force within the Board and, in 1897, Crooks was elected chairman.

The reforming Guardians first turned their attention to the Poor Law officials of whom Lansbury said the higher ones 'were paid large salaries to look after them (the poor)'.[13] He understood that the Poor Law system could brutalize even once-kindly officials for 'they soon discovered that the road to promotion and increased salaries was economy, at the expense of the poor'.[14] But this was no excuse for corruption. On examining the stores and the accounts, Lansbury and Crooks discovered that officials were buying stock inferior to what was recorded and pocketing the difference. The Local Government Board was reluctant to intervene for fear of a public scandal. The new Guardians insisted and the officials were sacked.

They then turned to conditions within the workhouse. Lansbury once inspected the porridge and found it:

> served with pieces of black stuff floating around. On examination we discovered it to be rat and mice manure. I called for the chief

officer, who immediately argued against me, saying the porridge was good and wholesome. 'Very good, Madam,' said I, taking up a basinful and spoon, 'here you are, eat one mouthful and I will acknowledge I am wrong.' 'Oh, dear no', said the fine lady, 'the food is not for me.'[15]

The food was improved, cocoa introduced, margarine replaced by butter and stale meat by fresh. Crooks then instigated a workhouse bakery which ensured both cheaper and better bread and more enjoyable tasks for some of the inmates. Next, the blue, ill-fitting uniform was abolished, as was the practice of separating elderly wives and husbands. Lansbury, Crooks and their colleagues were most unusual Guardians and, even as late as December 1910, the *Daily Telegraph* reported with some amazement that they had arranged for a pantomime to visit the workhouse where it was seen by 1,600 adults and children.

As a Guardian, Lansbury was also appointed a manager of Forest Gate District School, which was both a children's home and school serving the Poplar and Whitechapel Unions. He was appalled by its institutional regime, where children with shaven heads and drab uniforms spent most of their days within its walls before retiring to long dormitories. On becoming chairman, he abolished the seven-course dinners served by the children to the managers, appointed new and capable staff, introduced sporting activities, provided a wider range of vocational training and, eventually, sent the children out to ordinary day schools — and without their uniforms. Years later, by which time the school had been moved to Shenfield, it received a visit from Queen Mary. The children had been carefully coached about their behaviour before royalty but, when Lansbury appeared, they broke ranks and surged forward shouting, 'Good old George, good old George.'

Humanizing the institutions was not enough. The working-class Guardians wanted to keep people out of the workhouse altogether. They persuaded the Board to quadruple the inadequate amounts offered to old people and widows to survive in their own homes. During the economic depression of 1902–05, the workhouses were already full in Poplar, so the Guardians granted out-relief even to able-bodied men so that numbers on relief rose to 7,330 by 1906. Expenditure had to be met from the rate imposed by the Board and its increase provoked fierce criticism for Lansbury and Crooks. The reality, as Crowther explained, was that 'it cost more than three times as much merely to provide food, clothing and fuel for an indoor pauper as for an outdoor one'.[16] But this economic fact was lost on ratepayers who accused the Guardians of feather-bedding the poor in their own homes.

Meanwhile, Lansbury's concern about unemployment continued unabated. Within the Poor Law, he wanted to give inmates more constructive work. More importantly, he wanted to discover whether it was possible to equip them with skills for which there was a demand outside and whether it could actually create employment in order to stop people having to approach the Poor Law in the first place.

Lansbury had little money himself but at this juncture, in 1903, he met a wealthy American philanthropist, Joseph Fels, who frequently visited Britain. A self-made man, Fels never lost his support for working-class people and, although not a socialist, had great sympathies with the movement. In Fel's biography, his wife Mary told that 'one day he read a speech delivered by George Lansbury at a meeting of the Poplar Board. Its human note rang true and he immediately resolved to know the speaker.'[17] They soon met in Bow and, in a letter preserved in the Lansbury Collection, Lansbury recalled:

> I walked to the station with him, and before I left I came to feel that there was a kinship between us. During our conversation he impressed the fact on me that if he was to help the Poplar Board of Guardians, his name was to be kept quiet. This was so unusual for a rich man that it attracted me to him right away. On the station another incident occurred which struck me as unusual. When the train came in I asked him which class he was travelling, and like a shot came the reply, 'Third, because there isn't any fourth.'

For his part, Fels was drawn by Lansbury's sincerity, integrity and sense of humour. The Jewish businessman and the Christian socialist formed a friendship so firm that the latter described it 'as strong and loyal as that between Jonathan and David'.[18] When Fels was in London, they met daily. When away, Fels wrote regularly and, in a letter of 1906, he poked a little fun at Lansbury's religion, asked him to visit Mary who was still in Britain, and concluded, 'Whenever you have nothing better to do send me a line, even if on a postal card. Few men I care more to hold in touch with.'

In 1904, Fels purchased 100 acres of land at Laindon, Essex and persuaded the Local Government Board to allow the Poplar Board of Guardians to lease it for a peppercorn rent. The Guardians then sent 200 men who turned it into a farm of orchards and market gardens. The Guardians maintained the men's families but were not allowed to pay the men a wage, so Fels provided them with sixpence a week pocket money. The experiment won much publicity and, following a conference in Whitehall in October 1904, the *Local Government Journal* approvingly reported:

> Would it not be better instead of keeping men in workhouses, to polish brasses that did not want polishing, and scrub floors which did not want scrubbing, to take them into the country and try and train them for country life?

Lansbury used the publicity to obtain backing for a larger scheme. This time Fels lent £40,000, free of interest, for land at Hollesley Bay under the auspices of a number of local authorities brought together by the Central Unemployment Committee. The men again produced vegetables but this time were accompanied by their wives. Lansbury threw his energies into the scheme and visited regularly at weekends to give lectures and organize recreational activities.

Hollesley Bay, as will be shown, did not last long, and Laindon declined once the First World War created a demand for manpower. These schemes possessed two major limitations. They were small-scale affairs catering for a few hundred men whereas, in London alone, the unemployed numbered tens of thousands. Further, their design was such that they removed people from their familiar environments and, in the case of Laindon, separated men from their families. Understandably, some men found it difficult to cope without their wives, their children, their usual entertainments and their urban way of life.

On the other hand, the farms did provide work which was both useful and satisfying. Moreover, as the biographer of Will Crooks explains, once equipped with farm skills, some men found jobs on local farms while others emigrated to Canada.[19] Certainly, Lansbury regarded the schemes with satisfaction and in 1928 he wrote:

> It is no exaggeration to say that the despised Poplar Guardians

and Councillors can justly claim to be pioneers in constructive work for dealing with the unemployed.[20]

Lansbury could not claim that Poplar was the originator of such work, for some voluntary movements, particularly the Salvation Army, had also established farms and colonies. But, in an age when statutory intervention was generally regarded as unwarranted interference into economic matters, he and his colleagues were taking radical steps by winning statutory backing for such schemes of employment. Moreover, their steps were studied by others, for Laindon and Hollesley Bay were visited by other Boards of Guardians and other authorities which then set up similar schemes. Later, during the economic depression of the 1930s, central government itself accepted some responsibility — however limited — for providing jobs. Later still, in the 1980s, when unemployment levels exceeded even those of Lansbury's day, job training and job creation became major government programmes. These developments do owe something to Lansbury and his colleagues who argued not only that statutory bodies *should* intervene to create jobs but also demonstrated that they *could* do so.

The practices of the Poplar Guardians met with resistance from two sources. Locally, many ratepayers resented the money they spent on poor people. Centrally, leading Poor Law officials, backed by COS supporters, argued that they were undermining the spirit of the legislation of 1834. The resistance turned into outright attack when the Liberal government of 1906 appointed John Burns as president of the Local Government Board. Burns came from a working-class background but his early radicalism faded as he achieved high office and he sided with the chief Poor Law official, James Davey. Davey was a traditionalist determined to maintain the Poor Law practice of discouraging applications by ensuring that life inside the workhouse was no better than the meanest existence outside.

The Hollesley Bay colony came under direct central control and Burns converted it back into an old-style workhouse. Lansbury was furious but helpless. Burns then accepted the plea of Poplar ratepayers for an inquiry into the running of the Poplar Union and appointed Davey to conduct it. At the enquiry in 1906, a lawyer representing the Municipal Alliance — a mixture of Liberal and Conservative ratepayers — accused the Guardians of extravagance in buying best-quality food and not accepting the lowest tenders, of getting drunk at the ratepayers' expense, of packing the Laindon colony with criminals who terrorized the neighbourhood, and of having a former workhouse master, Madely, who took bribes from contractors. At the end of the day, Davey refused to allow Lansbury to reply immediately with the result that the next day's papers were full of the accusations.

Lansbury eventually replied with reason and incisiveness. He established that not only was the workhouse diet in accordance with the Local Government Board's own guidelines but also that its own inspectors had been visiting and approving expenditure. He then proved that no public money was spent on alcohol, a not surprising revelation given that the two leading Guardians, Lansbury and Crooks, were well-known teetotallers. He then questioned contractors to demonstrate that nothing illegal had occurred. One was verbally corrected so sharply by Lansbury that he cried out, 'Give me cold water,' adding, with more hope than expectation, 'I would like brandy after that.' Finally, Lansbury had to concede that Madely was pressurized to resign, not over any financial improbity but because of an affair with a workhouse nurse.

Crooks, when his turn came, detailed how the Guardians had got rid of corruption. He then drew upon figures to show that rises in expenditure dovetailed with rises in unemployment. Then, to Lansbury's surprise, a local officer of the COS spoke in praise of the Guardians' successful rehabilitation from the workhouse to the community of some inmates he had considered beyond redemption. Finally, the Guardian's legal representative prevailed upon two Essex policemen to admit that the Laindon colonists had committed little crime.

Davey's eventual report was, the historian Ryan says, one of 'strictest fairness'.[21] He made much of the amounts spent on workhouse supplies and of the lapses of Madely. He argued that the Guardians' liberal out-relief policy might encourage local employers to adopt a casual employment system knowing that any men they laid off could always depend upon the Poor Law. Certainly, he considered the humane and generous attitudes of the Guardians to be contrary to the intentions of Poor Law legislation. However, he had to admit of Lansbury and Crooks, 'There is most conclusive evidence that they . . . derived no personal profit from the existing system.'[22] Most tellingly, the report produced no grounds for the Local Government Board to take action against the Poplar Guardians.

The report did nothing to harm the standing of Lansbury and Crooks in Poplar and, in the following borough council elections, the Labour vote increased with Lansbury defeating the chairman of the Municipal Alliance. However, a number of the Guardians were worried by the tenor of Davey's report and hence became less amenable to the arguments of the socialist minority. Crooks resigned as chairman in 1907 to concentrate on his parliamentary duties and was replaced by a Municipal Alliance member. Consequently, the Board hardened some of its practices and cut back on expenditure on out-relief.

The Davey inquiry gained widespread publicity because Crooks and Lansbury were already recognized as leading Poor Law figures. Crooks won election to the Commons in 1903 and spoke frequently about the Poor Law. As early as 1895, Lansbury received an invitation to give evidence to the Royal Commission on the Aged Poor. One of its members, the famous social investigator Charles Booth, invited Lansbury to dinner the evening before he was due to appear. The workman Lansbury wrote, 'I had never been out to dinner before and of course possessed no dinner uniform, and never have done.'[23] The footmen treated him with disdain but the Booths put him at ease and Lansbury coped in his usual cheerful manner. The following day, he argued before the Commission that aged people should not be expected to work in workhouses, that they should be allowed to walk in and out as they wished and should be given better food and clothes. The Prince of Wales, who was also on the Commission, took up one of his points that inmates should have underclothes. Lansbury replied that the poor needed underclothes 'just like you and I do'. Later, the prince endorsed his plea for a more varied diet and suggested the addition of biscuits. Lansbury agreed but added that 'you will also have to supply them with teeth'.[24] The prince's agreement was then used by Lansbury for he promptly returned to Poplar and cited it as backing for improvements to the clothing and diet of the aged poor in its workhouse.

Ten years later, Lansbury himself was appointed to a Royal Commission on the Poor Laws set up, as one of its last acts, by the Conservative government in recognition that the principles and practices of 1834 might not be sufficient for the social problems of the twentieth century. Other members included a strong body from the COS, particularly Charles Loch, Helen Bosanquet and Octavia Hill, and the formidable Fabian, Beatrice Webb. Not surprisingly, when the Royal Commission finally reported in 1909 it was divided. The Majority Report by no means went along with Davey's desire to retain the Poor Law in its pure 1834 form. It wanted more emphasis on prevention and approved of the introduction of state old-age pensions and unemployment benefit for a limited number of people and it recommended the provision of labour exchanges to facilitate the finding of jobs. However, it wished to retain the Poor Law, merely transferring its system and institutions to local authority Public Assistance Committees instead of Boards of Guardians. The COS influence was seen in recommendations for more detailed scrutiny of applicants and for much greater involvement of Voluntary Aid committees in assessing them.

The Minority Report contained the signatures of Beatrice Webb, Prebendary (later Bishop) Russell Wakefield, the trade unionist Francis Chandler, and George Lansbury. It was, says Jean Heywood, the historian of services for deprived children, 'a burning piece of invective against what it stated was the failure of a destitution authority to relieve destitution, [it] recommended nothing less than the breaking up of the poor law and the transfer of its functions on a specialised basis to appropriate departments of the local authorities'.[25] In short, it wanted to do away with the Poor Law and its institutions and, instead, wanted responsibility for destitute children to pass from the Poor Law to local education authorities, for sick persons to health authorities, and for the elderly to pension committees. The first would give help without imparting stigma, the second would both restore people to working health and stop them having to enter insitutions marked out for paupers, and the third would enable the elderly poor to stay in their own homes.

Margaret Cole reflects the views of a number of commentators when she writes that the Minority Report 'takes rank as one of the great State Papers of this century'.[26] Cole, the biographer of Beatrice Webb, claims that Beatrice 'was almost entirely responsible for it although she received some help from Sydney in its drafting and writing'.[27] The reference to Sydney is to Beatrice's husband and Cole gives no credit to the other signatories of the Minority Report. No doubt, Beatrice was its main architect. Certainly, she perceived that Davey was feeding the Commission with evidence that supported his views. In response, she initiated a range of investigations which established that poverty was attributable to people's economic and social circumstances rather than to their individual laziness or wickedness. Yet Lansbury also made an important contribution. Unlike Beatrice, he knew about poverty from first hand and, unlike her, he had extensive experience as a Poor Law administrator. He was not the man to keep quiet at committee meetings and he later revealed that he was openly at odds with one of the well-to-do members who supported the principle of making workhouse life as mean as possible while insisting that he should have an enormous and secure income for himself.[28] Most tellingly of all, the recommendations of the Minority Report reflected the very points which Lansbury had been making for years. As early as 1897, he read a paper to the Central Poor Law Conference in which he argued that the workhouse perpetuated poverty, and he recommended that poverty be reduced by state-organized employment, that the elderly poor be kept out of the workhouse by pensions, and that Poor Law children be transferred to ordinary schools. Later, he called for the complete abolition of the Poor Law and the transfer of its functions to local authorities where services would be available as a right to all those in need. Lansbury must have fed these views into the Commission and, as occasional letters from Beatrice Webb reveal, she had a great respect for him.

Lansbury's influence became even more marked after the publication of the Report. Again, Margaret Cole portrays the Webbs as the flagbearers of the Minority Report. True, they were prominent members of the National Committee for the Break-up of the Poor Law, they spoke at Fabian meetings and wrote in what would now be called the quality press. But it was Lansbury, ably abetted by Will Crooks, who took the recommendations to the country as a whole. Immediately following publication of the Minority Report, Lansbury wrote a long article for the *Labour Leader*. He started by sympathizing with the Majority Report view that the Poor Law should be re-named Public Assistance and that its committees should be placed within local authorities. However, he took issue with its undemocratic provision that its committee members would be appointed by councils and hence might not be elected representatives of the people. He continued that the Majority Report was really continuing the stigma and deterrence of the old Poor Law under a new name. Instead, he — and the Minority Report — wanted extended local authority services which would enable people to cope within their own homes. He cleverly pointed out that Conservative politicians were always going on about the need to preserve family values and he concluded that his proposals

> would help to do what the anti-Socialists are constantly crying out that they want to do, but which they have never tried to do — that is, preserve home life.

The following year, in September 1910, Lansbury participated in a two-day conference in which Harry Quelch of the SDF accused him of being too moderate by concentrating on services rather than on the immediate abolition of poverty. The fact that the conference was well attended and all its proceedings published in a pamphlet testifies to the tremendous interest stimulated by the Minority Report. This interest continued for some years. In 1911, Lansbury published his booklet *Smash the Workhouse* and in February 1912 he devoted much of an article in the *Penny Pictorial* to ridiculing the middle-class myth that the workhouse was a soft option for the poor. He wrote: 'It is healthier to be born in the vilest slum in London than in a model workhouse.' To prove his point, he cited statistics to show that, while in London as a whole 132 out of 1,000 children died in the first year of life, in Poplar Workhouse it was between 268 and 302. He again concluded that the workhouse must go.

Lansbury thus devoted much time to promulgating the Minority Report. What did the Report achieve? In the short term, very little. The Liberal government was already introducing or discussing limited pensions, unemployment insurance and labour exchanges and so could easily accept the urgings of both Majority and Minority reports on these scores. John Burns, as Crowther explains, had not initiated the Royal Commission, tended to blame poverty on the failings of individuals and so 'saw little need for change'.[29] Consequently, the Liberal government made no moves to execute the main recommendations of either report. Yet Burns and his successors could not entirely ignore the critique of the Poor Law and, in the following years, some improvements were made to its operation. Regulations about out-door relief were rationalized, limits were set on the amount of time children aged under three could stay in the workhouse, greater attention was given to the medical care of inmates and, in 1913, the term 'workhouse' was officially replaced by 'Poor Law institution'. But not until the

Local Government Act of 1929 were the duties of Guardians taken over by local authority Public Assistance Committees. As late as 1939 Public Assistance institutions still contained nearly 100,000 inmates, while in 1946 examples could be found of small children residing alongside the elderly and the mentally ill in what were still called the workhouses.

In the long term, however, the Minority Report became a cornerstone of the future welfare state: social reformers made continual references to its analysis of the failings of the Poor Law and to its plea for broader based, non-stigmatizing services. The Minority Report stressed the need for state welfare benefits to prevent the destitution which forced people into the workhouse. Gradually, if grudgingly, pensions, sickness payments and unemployment benefits were introduced by the state and so ensured some limited forms of cover in times of old age, illness and unemployment. The Report argued for local authority services which would be specialized in function yet general in the sense of not being restricted to paupers. Throughout the inter-war years, local authority health, education and housing services were slowly established. The Report reasoned that the relief of immediate poverty should be a central government not a parish responsibility and, in time, the creation of the Unemployment Assistance Board signalled a trend in that direction. Not until 1946 did the National Assistance Act contain the memorable words, 'The existing poor law shall cease to have effect,' and not until that decade of the 1940s were the National Health Service, the National Assistance Board and the local authority Children's Departments added to the modern welfare state. Yet they all rested on principles of prevention and universalism laid down in the Minority Report — a report to which Lansbury as well as Beatrice Webb made a significant contribution.

The experience of being a member of the Royal Commission also had a significant impact on Lansbury. He studied poverty in depth, by reading hundreds of documents, listening to many witnesses and visiting scores of institutions. He concluded:

I came from the Commission a more convinced Socialist than when I started. My conviction grows stronger as the years pass that everything we do on palliative lines leaves some evil behind it, and that there is no remedy for poverty and destitution except the total and complete abolition of the causes which produce these evils, and that in the main, though there are many individual exceptions, these evils are social and not personal.[30]

Lansbury's connection with the Poor Law did not end with the Royal Commission. He remained a Guardian for as long as that office existed. In August 1918, the staff of the Poplar Poor Law institutions presented him with cutlery to mark his twenty-five years as a Guardian. He must have been moved by their respect and affection, which contrasted with the resentment and hostility of their predecessors a quarter of a century before. A local newspaper reported him replying with these words:

> Our work in Poplar has been a labour of love. We did it because we could no other, and we trust that in the day to come our children and their children will, with the men and women of their day, enjoy a happier and fuller life because of the work our friends and ourselves have tried to do.

These were no empty words, for it certainly was 'a labour'. As a Guardian, Lansbury attended weekly or fortnightly meetings plus a host of sub-committees. In addition, he often went at weekends to Poor Law conferences and spent time writing and campaigning for reform. Moreover, it was 'a labour of love' for there were no perks to be gained. Guardians received no payments. When Lansbury started, many poor people did not possess the franchise so there were few votes to be won for council and parliamentary elections. On the contrary, his insistence on extra expenditure to improve the workhouses provoked the ire of ratepayers who did have the vote. Further, as Davey noticed in his report on the Poplar Guardians, Lansbury was unusual in being a Guardian who lived among the very people who feared yet had to turn to the Poor Law. Frequently they knocked upon his door, pleading with him to help prevent them from going to the workhouse. Lansbury accepted all these pressures because he cared passionately about the lot of those deemed to be 'paupers'. In 1920 Lansbury exhorted others to:

> go back to the lonely Nazarene, learn of Him and, learning, understand that wealth and power, majesty and glory are no worth, that no lasting happiness comes from great possessions, but instead, that today, yesterday and forever the only gospel whereby man can be saved from the power of evil is contained

in the words, 'He who would be the greatest amongst you must be the servant of all' — and not servant in order to rule but to serve.[31]

In penning these words, Lansbury was not thinking of the Poor Law; nevertheless they reflect the role he adopted, for he saw the position of Guardian not as a means to status and power but as being a servant to the poorest. Interestingly, Edgar Lansbury judged that his father 'spent his most thrilling, if not his greatest days as a humble member of a Board of Guardians'.[32]

Lansbury devoted a lifetime to being a Guardian. Above all, he insisted on trying to use his position for the good of poor people. Many Guardians regarded the Poor Law merely as a means of deterring or even punishing them. Some socialists deemed it an instrument of class oppression and so refused to have anything to do with it. Lansbury agreed that it was an evil institution but, as long as it survived, he determined to improve it. Undoubtedly, he and his colleagues did humanize the workhouse, did extend out-relief and did initiate schemes to succour the unemployed. In addition, they did improve the educational facilities and care of Poor Law children. Harold Laski called the school they established at Shenfield 'the great poor law school which is a model to every public authority in England', and he continued about Lansbury:

> Go with him to Shenfield, and the simple happiness of its children merely because he is there is as moving a sight as there is to be seen in England.[33]

In raising the standards of the Poor Law, Lansbury and his fellow Guardians did contribute to a remarkable change. As Clem Attlee put it in 1937:

> It is hardly realised by many in the movement today how much was accomplished by men like Lansbury and Crooks in revolutionising the ideas of the people with regard to Poor Law administration.[34]

Additionally, as a Poor Law administrator, Lansbury was influential in proclaiming a different way of regarding poor people. He declared:

I am quite aware some people are bad and deceitful. I know this because I know myself. I know people drink, gamble, and are often lazy. I also know that taken in the mass the poor are as decent as any other class.[35]

It was because he regarded poor people as decent people that Lansbury wanted decent services for them. He believed that if human beings were treated brutally then they became brutal but if treated humanely they became humane. Gradually this view gained ground and did shape subsequent central and local government social services.

Contemporary newspapers and politicians paid many tributes to Lansbury the Guardian. However, it was not praise that motivated him. Rather it was the plight of people like Mr Munroe of Bethnal Green who earned six shillings a week selling glasses but whose rent amounted to seven shillings and nine pence. In a letter of 1909, which Lansbury preserved, Munroe wrote to him:

There is not much left now, and I cannot live on the kindness of friends for an indefinite period and must soon . . . apply to the poor law authorities; that is a prospect that I view with horror and dread . . . I know it will break my wife's heart to be parted from her children, especially the baby boy.

I have often thought of suicide as the only way out of it, but that would mean that I must also take the lives of those dependent on me, and I feel that I can not bring myself to that. When people become same as you and others like you are in the House of Commons, instead of the rotters who are there now, the future will be brighter, there will then be no careworn, haggard fathers and mothers, no hungry little ones imploring for food but happiness and plenty for all.

References

1   M.A. Crowther, *The Workhouse System 1834–1929*, Batsford Academic, 1981.

2   N. Middleton, *When Family Failed*, Gollancz, 1971, p. 65.

3   G. Lansbury, *My Life*, Constable, 1928, pp. 135–36.

4   G. Lansbury, *Looking Backwards and Forwards*, Blackie and Son, 1935, pp. 228–29.

5   W. Fishman, *East End 1888*, Duckworth, 1988, pp. 258–62.

6   Cited in Mrs Barnardo and J. Marchant, *Memoirs of the Late Dr Barnardo*, Hodder and Stoughton, 1907, pp. 242–43.

7   Cited in B. Holman, *Putting Families First*, Macmillan Education, 1988, p. 12.

8   J. Pimlott, *Toynbee Hall*, Dent & Co., 1935, p. 152.

9   Lansbury, *Looking Backwards*, p. 205.

10 Lansbury, *My Life*, p. 129.

11 Ibid., p. 132.

12 Crowther, *The Workhouse System*, p. 79.

13 Lansbury, *Looking Backwards*, p. 200.

14 Ibid., p. 202.

15 Lansbury, *My Life*, pp. 136–37.

16 Crowther, *The Workhouse System*, p. 59.

17 M. Fels, *The Life of Joseph Fels*, Doubleday, Doran & Co., 1940, p. 53.

18 Lansbury, *Looking Backwards*, p. 223.

19 G. Haw, *From Workhouse to Westminster: The Life Story of Will Crooks*, Cassell & Co., reprinted 1909, p. 267.

20 Lansbury, *My Life*, p. 146.

21 P. Ryan, 'Poplarism 1894–1930', in P. Thane (ed.), *The Origins of British Social Policy*, Croom Helm, 1978, p. 68.

22 Cited in R. Postgate, *The Life of George Lansbury*, Longmans, Green & Co., 1951, p. 68.

23 Lansbury, *My Life*, p. 139.

24 Ibid., p. 140.

25 J. Heywood, *Children in Care*, Routledge and Kegan Paul, 1959, p.111.

26 M. Cole, *Beatrice Webb*, Longmans, Green & Co., second edition, 1946, p. 99.

27 Ibid., p. 89.

28 Lansbury, *Looking Backwards*, pp. 202–03.

29 Crowther, *The Workhouse System*, p. 86.

30 Lansbury, *My Life*, p. 153.

31 G. Lansbury, *These Things Shall Be*, Swarthmore Press, 1920, p. 15.

32   E. Lansbury, *George Lansbury, My Father*, Sampson Low, Marston & Co., 1934, p. 47.

33   H. Laski, Introduction to G. Lansbury, *My Life*, reissued 1931, pp. ix and xi.

34   C. Attlee, *The Labour Party in Perspective*, Gollancz, 1937, p. 31.

35   Lansbury, *My Life*, p. 133.

4
ELECTED TO PARLIAMENT

Following the Report of the Royal Commission on the Poor Laws in 1909, Lansbury toured the country to publicize the recommendations of the Minority Report. Soon he was also electioneering. In the general election of January 1910, he was defeated at Bow and Bromley. However, the Liberal government, locked in conflict with the Conservative-dominated House of Lords, went to the country again in December. This time Lansbury gained victory over his Conservative opponent, a victory which owed something to the intervention of David Lloyd George who urged Liberals to vote for Lansbury.

Lansbury, one of forty-two Labour MPs, made his maiden speech in February 1911, a few days before his fifty-second birthday. The speech, 'The Right to Work', contained three features typical of much of what he wrote and said at this time. He graphically drew attention to the plight of poor people:

> We have had lots of sympathy this afternoon; but sympathy is not of much use to the children who are selling newspapers, or riding behind vans, or sleeping on the Embankment or workhouses or casual wards.

Then he turned attention from the poor to the rich by arguing that:

> when I deal with the loafers I will deal with those who canter round Rotten Row for want of any other exercise to obtain an appetite for their meals. If ever the democracy of this country deal with loafers, they will deal with them at both ends of the scale.

Lastly, he made the case for state intervention to support the poor:

If you deny men the right to work, if you take from them by your capitalist and landlord system the means of earning their daily bread, you cannot at the same time deny their claim to maintenance at the hands of the state.

In 1910, Britain's new monarch George V led an empire which covered a quarter of the globe's land surface and which was protected by the strongest navy in the world. At the end of that year, his prime minister, Herbert Asquith, and a cabinet which included David Lloyd George, John Burns and Winston Churchill, faced five main issues. First, Germany was challenging Britain as an economic power and also pursuing its claims for an empire which would provide raw materials and an outlet for trade. Britain became the more determined to hold on to its colonies while both sides began to increase the size of their armed forces. Lansbury's views were at odds with those of most MPs. Not only did he deplore any extra expense on the army and navy, he also advocated that India should be governed by its own people. His stance is the more amazing if it is remembered that, as McLean explained, most public figures 'shared the view that "natives" were inferior, unreliable people . . . who could not possibly rule each other'.[1] Lansbury dismissed such judgments as inconsistent with his Christianity which held that God created all people of equal worth. Henceforth, his home in the East End received a constant stream of visitors and letters from India.

The second question was that of Irish Home Rule. British parliaments had long been split over Ireland, where a strong movement for Home Rule frequently erupted into violence. Lansbury had visited Ireland, was appalled at the poverty and the harshness of landlords, and sided with the Home Rulers.

The third issue concerned the House of Lords. The Liberal government was determined to curb the powers of the non-elected House of Lords. Eventually, the Parliament Act of 1911 did replace its legislative veto by delaying powers only. Lansbury agreed with the legislative action and, indeed, was opposed to the whole idea of a hereditary chamber.

Lansbury thus contributed to the above three issues. But the remaining two — benefits for the poor and votes for women — were even more important to him. His views on these subjects caused some differences with his Labour colleagues and eventually led to his resignation from the Commons.

In the early twentieth century, Britain was still a country where the enormous wealth of some existed alongside the abject poverty of others. A tiny proportion of the population — just 0.5 per cent — owned 65.5 per cent of the capital while 2.5 per cent received two thirds of the national income. Yet the mass of workers earned less than £160 a year and 30 per cent of people lived on or below a meanly drawn poverty line. At least, a growing number of workers were represented by trade unions whose overall membership had risen to over four million. With unemployment increasing and real wages falling, the unions engaged in some bitter disputes which led, in some instances, to the government's sending in troops to control strikers.

The dual desire to relieve poverty and to dampen industrial discontent prompted the Liberals into social legislation. Already in 1908 it had brought in pensions for a limited number of over-seventy-year-olds. Then, in 1911, it introduced the National Insurance Bill which contained two major parts. Health insurance was proposed for low earners: workers, employers and the state would make weekly contributions which entitled certain workers to medical treatment and sickness benefits for a limited period. A similar tripartite contribution concerned unemployment insurance which merited unemployment pay for, again, a limited period for some two-and-a-quarter million workers.

A number of Labour MPs supported the bill. Lansbury, who always contested the view that the Liberal government was a reformist one, vehemently opposed it. He argued that the Labour movement had always held that unemployment and health benefits should be financed wholly from taxation. He denounced the workers' contribution as a poll tax which took money out of the already low wages of workers. He added that the employers would just put their contribution on to the price of goods which were largely purchased by the working classes. The insurance idea was, in his view, a con trick by which employees had to pay for their own benefits so that the wealthy would have to pay less in income tax.

Conservatives opposed the bill for different reasons. They believed it gave too much away. But their and Lansbury's arguments were of no avail. Lloyd George had an appealing slogan, 'Ninepence for fourpence' — on the grounds that the insured gained nine pence for every four pence they paid in. The bill won the approval of country and parliament.

Despite the defeat, Lansbury sustained his attacks upon the government. He was constantly on his feet to protest at the treatment of the deprived and to contrast it with that given to the privileged. He initiated a bill, which had no chance of success, to give workers a holiday with pay. He used the Commons as a platform to defend strikers who were prosecuted for distributing 'Don't Shoot' leaflets to soldiers. Lloyd George sneeringly remarked that Lansbury had become the leader of the opposition. The sneer hurt Ramsay MacDonald, who already considered that Lansbury was lacking in party discipline. Their differences were to widen over an issue so important to Lansbury that Postgate said it 'even eclipsed for a while his devotion to socialism'.[2] The issue was women's suffrage.

During the nineteenth century, women had obtained the vote in local elections and the right to sit on school boards, on the Boards of Guardians and, in 1907, on local councils. Yet they were still denied the vote in parliamentary elections. Pressure for reform came most strongly from two organizations. The moderate National Union of Women's Suffrage Societies (NUWSS) was led by Mrs Fawcett. The more militant suffragettes belonged to the Women's Social and Political Union (WSPU) founded in 1903 by Mrs Emmeline Pankhurst and her daughters, Christabel and Sylvia. In addition, within the Labour Party the Women's Labour League campaigned, as Margaret Bondfield recalled, 'to obtain direct Labour representation of women in Parliament'.[3] But, being confined to the Labour ranks, it never achieved the national impact of the main two bodies.

Lansbury was not jumping on the bandwagon of the women's campaign in 1910. In the 1880s he had spoken at women's meetings, calling for their right to be local authority councillors. He gave enthusiastic support to the suffragettes and, unlike many in the movement, perceived that women were economically as well as politically oppressed. To be economically independent, mothers needed day care for their children and Lansbury became chairman of a body, the Day Nurseries for the Children of Working Mothers, which initiated day nurseries in London. Its campaign provoked the wrath of some middle-class women who complained that such mothers would neglect the 'home training' of their offspring. Lansbury replied sharply in the *Daily News* of 10 July 1905, by pointing out that the same middle classes 'left their children with nurses or governesses'. Once more, Lansbury's social belief stemmed from his Christianity, for he held that men and women were equal in the sight of God and that, therefore, one sex should not be superior to another. However, he readily admitted that many other Christians did not share his interpretation and so he castigated a so-called Christian country which allowed women, particularly working-class women, to be oppressed socially and economically. He just could not understand how Christian people could tolerate conditions and systems which sent women to the workhouse. Writing of a starving woman who knocked at his door, he stated, 'I can't find it in my heart to say to her that she is my sister in the sight of God . . . so she passes on, indifferent to our creed which to her is meaningless.' He continued, 'To me the most important question for the Christians of England to consider is this condition-of-women question.'[4]

George's election to the Commons coincided with a period when the WSPU was pursuing more militant tactics which brought it into open conflict with the authorities. He was then outraged at the latter's heavy-handed response. From letters smuggled to him from suffragettes in Holloway Prison, he heard first hand of their rough treatment and, when they went on hunger strikes, of the horrors of forcible feeding. With Keir Hardie, Lansbury frequently questioned the prime minister about these matters and was disgusted at the accompanying chauvinistic jokes and loutish behaviour of some MPs.

On 25 June 1912, Asquith was questioned about the 'torture' of woman prisoners. He replied that the women had only to undertake not to break the law outside in order to leave prison. His uncaring and arrogant tone provoked Lansbury to fury. He later recorded:

> This so infuriated me that I rushed down the House in a white heat of passion, shouting to him that what he was saying was exactly what every tyrant said who had put reformers in prison; that he knew perfectly well none of these women, because of their creed and faith, could submit to the conditions which he laid down.[5]

Lansbury was white with anger, Asquith red with embarrassment.

Members leapt to their feet and the Speaker ordered Lansbury to leave. Subsequently, he was suspended temporarily from the Commons.

Lansbury's behaviour led to condemnation from most newspapers and criticism from Ramsay MacDonald. Yet, to his amazement, it also made him a virtual hero. Nothing he did ever produced such a flood of letters and telegrams. In the Lansbury Collection, 427 pages are covered with them. Not surprisingly, many came from suffragettes, such as a WSPU member who wrote:

> May God bless, preserve and prosper you for your magnificent bravery in defending women in a place where they have no possibility of defending themselves.

Others came from women who were not members but who believed in the cause. A number were penned by Conservative women, by teachers and doctors. Letters arrived from South Africa, from the United States, and one from a missionary in Kapar who signed herself 'A solitary suffragette'. Letters on society notepaper, letters scrawled in pencil on scraps of paper, hundreds of women (and some men) thanked Lansbury for making a stand for women's rights.

Buoyed by this display of support, Lansbury then took the drastic step of resigning his seat in order to stand again at the by-election. He explained himself with these words:

> I left the House of Commons on October, 1912, because of disagreement with the Party on the subject of the franchise. The Government had declared its intention of bringing in what would to all intents and purposes have been a Manhood Suffrage Bill. I proposed that the Party should move an amendment to that bill and vote against it unless women were included. It was a question on which I felt it impossible to compromise. I consulted my friends at Bow and they supported me in my point of view, and also took the view that I was responsible to them and not to the Party in the House of Commons.[6]

Lansbury fought the election on the issue of women's rights. In his manifesto, still preserved in the Lansbury Collection, he wrote:

> The women of our country live hard laborious lives. Down

here, where I have lived almost all my years, I have grown
to understand in some small way what poverty and destitution
mean to the women. We men have wanted to use our votes to
improve our social condition. I want that our mothers, our wives
and our sisters should be allowed to join us in the fight.

He had anticipated a victory that would then encourage the
Labour Party to support his tactic in the Commons. Instead, he
lost the election by 731 votes. He had miscalculated the mood of
his constituency, where many working-class voters felt that the
suffragette leaders — who had campaigned with Lansbury — were
middle-class women with little genuine sympathy for socialism, the
socialism for which they had sent Lansbury to the Commons. The
socialist solicitor, Saunders Jacobs, wrote to Lansbury and bluntly
explained that, although the women's cause was righteous, their
organization was 'using you as a tool' for ends which were not
socialist. Years later, Lansbury admitted of his resignation, 'It was
not a wise political decision.'[7]

The decision by Lansbury to risk his seat may seem all the more
puzzling in that, despite Ramsay MacDonald's dislike of his lack of
parliamentary discipline, he seemed set for advancement within the
party. His speeches in and out of the House were establishing his
political reputation. Keir Hardie, reporting a Labour conference in
the *Merthyr Pioneer* in 1911, had reflected his growing stature:

Lansbury has the frame of a giant and the frank, open face of
a healthy, happy schoolboy. In a very few sentences he had
gripped the Conference and as he went on the Conference kept
responding in a growing degree of sympathy with the man and
his message.

Yet by resigning and losing, Lansbury annoyed his parliamentary
colleagues, lost the sympathy of many Labour supporters, and, at
the age of fifty-three, seemed to have ended any hopes of ever
holding office in a government.

So what lay behind Lansbury's resignation? Apart from the
immediate issue of the Manhood Suffrage Bill, his decision was
probably influenced by some disillusionment both with the Labour
Party and with parliament itself. A number of Labour MPs,
especially those with trade union backing, favoured close links with
the Liberal government and pointed out that it had passed several

reforms beneficial to working people, including the Payment of Members Act of 1911 which helped MPs like Lansbury to receive a regular income. MacDonald would have no truck with formal Lib-Lab alliance but was prepared to support certain bills in order to obtain legislation to confirm the right of trade unions to collect a political levy from their members. By contrast, Lansbury wanted no compromises with the government until it concentrated on such major issues as votes for women and the abolition of the Poor Law. He wanted the parliamentary Labour Party to be seen as a socialist party which would not make trade-offs with the capitalists. His forthright views widened the gap between him and the Labour leadership.

Further, Lansbury was experiencing, for the only time in his life, some doubts about the institution of parliament itself. He could not see how all women would ever get the vote if it depended upon the decision of an all-male legislature. Going further, he pondered whether a middle-class institution would ever support real socialism. On 17 May 1912, he wrote in the *Labour Leader*:

> I have come to see that national organisation through a Parliament such as that at Westminster is of all things the most hopeless for the workers, and I cannot help feeling that in the future we will have to depend for real democracy on the spontaneous will of the common people . . . I have much more faith that the workers themselves will work out their salvation by organised industrial effort than by trusting to the middle and upper classes for the supply of experts to manage them.

This statement shows sympathy for a movement, much favoured by radical socialists of the time, called syndicalism, which stressed the potential of workers using industrial weapons, such as strikes, to secure political ends. To be sure, in the end Lansbury did not abandon his belief in the Labour Party and the Commons and the next chapter will show how he defended both against the arguments of those who pressed the case for violence and revolution. But, for a short while, he had his doubts. Hence the possible loss of his parliamentary seat and the approval of other Labour MPs weighed less heavily upon him.

Out of the Commons, Lansbury remained as active as ever. He supported several strikes and organized relief for the hungry families of strikers. He continued both as a Guardian and in agitating for reform of the Poor Law: he served as a borough councillor and, as will be shown, took a leading part in founding the *Daily Herald*.

His greatest commitment, however, stayed with the cause of women. He toured the country speaking on their behalf and, in London, facilitated the work of the Pankhursts. On one occasion Sylvia Pankhurst, who had been legally forbidden to address public gatherings, hid in the Lansbury home prior to a meeting at Bow Baths. When the police surrounded the house, Lansbury's daughter, Daisy, walked out dressed in Sylvia's clothes. While she was being arrested, George and Sylvia escaped to the meeting. Having made their speeches, they discovered that the police were waiting outside. Women in the audience pooled their clothing and produced six Sylvia Pankhursts. As the six were being rounded up by the baffled police, the genuine article slipped away.

Many women went to prison, and before long George followed. On 10 April 1913, at a huge rally in the Albert Hall, he implied that the militant tactic of destroying property was acceptable providing no life was endangered. In court, Lansbury was charged with seditious speech and ordered to find two sureties of £500 and to keep the peace for twelve months. On refusing, he was sent to prison for three months. In Pentonville Jail, he promptly went on hunger strike and a young chaplain rebuked him for defiling the temple of the Holy Ghost, the body. Lansbury referred him to Latimer and Ridley, clergymen martyrs of the Reformation era who allowed their temples to be destroyed by fire rather than submit themselves to unjust laws. Lansbury wryly recorded, 'The young man cleared out without saying another word.'[8] Meanwhile, the crowds protesting on Lansbury's behalf were so large that he could hear their cheers from his cell. Embarrassed by his hunger strike and alarmed by the demonstrations, the government gave way and within a few days released Lansbury to a welcoming throng of thousands.

The WSPU was an undemocratic body, dominated by the Pankhursts, middle class in tone and militant in tactics. Lansbury's backing for it rather than the more democratic NUWSS, which was firmly opposed to any forms of violence, puzzled some contemporaries. Postgate reasons that it was the state's treatment of the former — who were not properly protected from aggressive crowds by the police, who were imprisoned for minor offences such as stone throwing, who were subjected to forcible feeding in prison — which so enraged Lansbury that he developed a 'complete obsession' for their side.[9] Two other factors must be added. First, he probably reckoned that the WSPU, with its dynamic leadership and flair for publicity had a better chance of success than the more insipid NUWSS. Further, he hoped to broaden the programme of the WSPU. Thus, at one of their rallies, on 28 June 1912, he explained that his aim was to extend the vote to all adults — to those men still without the vote, and to working-class as well as middle-class women. He must have been gratified when Sylvia Pankhurst moved to live in the East End and when her East London Federation became more and more a socialist movement. This development, however, displeased the other Pankhursts who eventually broke with Sylvia and, indeed, had little to do with Lansbury after the 1912 by-election.

What was Bessie Lansbury's attitude to and involvement in the campaign? Bessie was very careful about her relationships with middle-class women and apparently took pains not to be drawn away from her working-class friendships and not to needlessly avail herself of privileges that her neighbours could not enjoy. Interestingly, the Lansbury Collection contains a number of letters from well-to-do female socialists, particularly Mrs Coates Hansen, urging her to enjoy holidays and travel abroad with them. She never went. She was a strong supporter of votes for women and a receipt shows that she was a member of the WSPU from at least 1907. However, she seems to have shared some of the common working-class mistrust of its middle-class leadership. Why had the Pankhursts formed the WSPU at all when close to their original Manchester base had been the more working-class North of England Society, which was already running a votes campaign? It seemed as though the Pankhursts would only participate if they led the movement. Further, as the Lansbury's son Edgar explained, Bessie 'resented their coming into Bow and sidetracking the enthusiasm of the growing movement for Socialism into an agitation for votes for women which in her view was always a subsidiary issue'.[10] Bessie feared that the suffragettes, some of whom wanted votes just for women property-owners, might alienate socialist supporters in the East End. Patricia Romero's biography of Sylvia Pankhurst gives some justification to that fear, and she records a councillor Thorne of Poplar accusing Sylvia and her top-drawer friends of having 'no more sympathy with the people of Bow and Bromley than they have with the people of Africa'.[11] In fact, Sylvia did embrace socialism and Bessie worked more closely with her especially during the 1914–18 War in community projects to help local families suffering because of separation from their men and because of food and fuel shortages. Subsequently, however, Sylvia took up communism and rejected both the Labour Party and the Lansburys. Thus, in 1923, speaking for the Unemployed Workers' Organisation, she accused Lansbury of doing the work of the capitalists in his role of Guardian. Still later she left communism and finally settled in Ethiopia and devoted her life to supporting a feudal monarchy. Meanwhile, Bessie stayed in Bow campaigning both for votes for women and for socialism.

Bessie and George must have felt their contribution was worthwhile when the Representation of the People Act of 1918 extended votes to many but not all women. By this time, the steam had gone out of the WSPU and neither it nor Lansbury could claim to be the main influence upon the final legislation. Nonetheless, Lansbury had given much to the women's cause. For a while, he was their foremost supporter in the House of Commons. In the country at large, he frequently spoke at well-attended meetings. In the East End, he recruited many women into the movement and, on one occasion, took the initiative of arranging for a deputation of working-class women to put their case at 10 Downing Street, an unusual measure in those days. In the Labour Party, he had some success in popularizing his conviction that the improvement to women's social and economic position — as well as getting the vote — was a legitimate part of socialism.

Throughout these years, George Lansbury's Christianity was at the forefront of his thinking and practice. He frequently chaired and spoke at Christian gatherings, particularly those of the Church Socialist League. In 1912, although a busy MP, he accepted the invitation of a Rev. Barry to address a meeting because, as the local Halifax paper reported him as saying, 'When a minister stood out for Labour it was the duty of all the Labour movement to stand by that minister.'

Lansbury believed that Christians, whether or not they were socialists, should be concerned about the social conditions of others. Thus, at the Halifax meeting, he declared that:

when the working people of the country understood the true
Christian theory of life — which was that every human being
was of equal value in the sight of God with every other — they
would not be content with the present conditions in which their

women lived, and they would not be content to let their children go into the mills and factories at 12 or 13 years of age.

Further, he wanted Christians to support and co-operate with socialists. In May 1911, at a meeting of the Church Socialist League, he stated:

> I want to see the Christian men and women joining with the Labour people in proclaiming to all men and women this, which to me is an unalterable truth, that 'One is our Father' and we are all brothers and sisters. If instead of thinking each for himself we did as Christ did, and think of others this would be a place of beauty and a place of joy.

Indeed, he was now arguing that the Christian ideal of brotherhood and sisterhood needed a social system which facilitated its practice — and that system was socialism. But, he continued in the same talk, socialism 'without religious enthusiasm . . . will become as selfish and soulless as any other movement that has cursed the world'. In short, Lansbury believed that Christianity needed socialism and that socialism needed Christianity.

Unlike some contemporary socialists, Lansbury did not regard Christianity just as the ethical base for socialism. He gained personal strength, and perhaps that inner peace which others noted, by worship in church. Again in the London talk, he explained how:

> often away on a Sunday . . . church had a magnetic attraction for me. I never go merely to hear the preacher . . . I like to feel that at any rate there is some communion between me and what I cannot see but what I feel is around and above me.

But even church was not always sufficient. Sometimes in his worship he felt he was getting nowhere. He went on to say that

> it is good in these conditions to get apart and rest just a little while, and remember that whatever you may say about Him and His Message, there was someone who lived 2000 years ago, who went through this world bearing the burden of sin and sorrow in His life and that He too lived weary days, He too lived a hard life and often a life of depression. But He left with mankind this message, He left with you and me this ideal,

that 'One is our Father' and that through Christ we approach Him.

Lansbury needed his faith to sustain him during these years. Apart from the trauma of losing his parliamentary seat and going to prison, his financial situation, although never as bad as in his earlier years, again gave cause for some anxiety. Having given up the wood mill firm, George relied on his journalistic earnings until the introduction of a modest salary for MPs brought a brief respite. Even so, in January 1912, Bessie was again taking out a loan for seventy-five pounds. Then, in 1913, two of their children were imprisoned. Annie, aged thirty, received a month's hard labour after being convicted, with others, of damaging a window in Bow following a meeting of the WSPU. William got two months' hard labour after breaking a window at Bromley Town Hall as an anti-government gesture. George, more worried about these sentences than over his own imprisonment, wrote to the Home Office and obtained a remission of the hard labour component for all those convicted. Their imprisonment led to letters of sympathy and encouragement from a number of friends. Commissioner David Lamb of the Salvation Army, who had great respect and affection for Lansbury, wrote

> I can understand the deep feelings of revolt against existing conditions. I have been through it all — May Christ the Master be near to them and you.

Annie and Willie survived prison and family life remained close and strong. George and Bessie were proud of Dorothy (often called Dolly) as she spoke at political meetings, particularly on women's issues, and of Edgar who joined his father as an elected member of Poplar Borough Council. In 1912, Dolly married Ernest Tuttle and the couple emigrated to the United States. Joseph Fels then persuaded George to do a lecture tour in that country. No doubt, George and Bessie went not just to preach socialism, but also because it gave them the opportunity to see the couple again. Soon afterwards, Edgar, aged twenty-six, married Minnie Glassman, a strong socialist and supporter of women's rights. The year was 1914, the date of the start of the First World War.

References

1. I. McLean, *Keir Hardie*, Allen Lane, 1975, p. 130.

2. R. Postgate, *The Life of George Lansbury*, Longmans, Green & Co., 1951, p. 117.

3. M. Bondfield, *A Life's Work*, Hutchinson & Co., 1948, p. 124.

4. G. Lansbury, chapter in G. Haw (ed.), *Christianity and the Working Classes*, Macmillan and Co., 1906, pp. 171–72.

5. G. Lansbury, *My Life*, Constable, 1928, p. 118.

6. Ibid., pp. 120–21.

7. G. Lansbury, *Looking Backwards and Forwards*, Blackie and Son, 1935, p. 98.

8. Lansbury, *My Life*, p. 123.

9. Postgate, *Life of George Lansbury*, p. 119.

10. E. Lansbury, *George Lansbury, My Father*, Sampson Low, Marston & Co., 1934, p. 140.

11. P. Romero, *E. Sylvia Pankhurst*, Yale University Press, 1987, p. 77.

5

PACIFIST AND PUBLICIST

On 14 August 1914, Britain declared war on Germany and so entered the First World War. The Labour Party was divided. MacDonald courageously declared in the Commons that Britain should have remained neutral. However, the majority of the party, in and out of parliament, backed the government and MacDonald resigned the leadership to be replaced by Arthur Henderson.

Lansbury, like Ramsay Macdonald and Keir Hardie, had mistakenly believed that many working-class men would refuse to take up arms against fellow workers of other nations. Hardie was shouted down in his own constituency and died in 1915. Lansbury had to continue despite the jeers that he favoured 'the Hun'. At least he had the experience of being a pacifist (although the word itself was not common until this period) during the intense jingoism of the Boer War in 1899–1901. Then, as a leading member of the International Crusade Against War, he had been spat upon, vilified and physically assaulted. No hardships could alter his view, for pacifism was one of his core beliefs, and, years later, was to cost him the leadership of the Labour Party.

Lansbury was not a pacifist by temperament. As a young man, his temper was easily aroused, and his powerful physique lent power to his fists. His pacifism followed from his Christianity. He reasoned that:

> killing any human being . . . must be wrong if we believe in the incarnation, for are we not taught that because Christ Himself became flesh, therefore all life is sacred?[1]

He reinforced his argument by drawing attention to the example of Christ who refused to use violence even when subjected to it.

76

Lastly, he exhorted others to copy 'the example of those early Christians who for three centuries endured terrible persecution and death rather than join in the mass murder of their fellow men and women[2].

Lansbury was sometimes accused of being 'too simple' in his condemnation of war and of offering no ways to stop war. He would probably have accepted the former judgment for, in some ways, his was a child-like faith which accepted that the example of the Galilean, as he loved to call Christ, could be applied to the complexities of the twentieth century. The second judgment is less fair, for Lansbury constantly wrote about the paths to peace. He reasoned that fear was the basis of war, fear that a rival country would gain more economic power. Such fear, he held, was unnecessary, for the abundance of the earth contained raw materials and markets sufficient for all. Lansbury therefore constantly called for conferences and international agreements to share the abundance. It was fear that led nations to increase their armaments and he rightly predicted that the rearmament programmes of Britain and Germany would inevitably reach the point where the arms would be used. He continually advocated the reduction of British arms on the grounds that it would lessen the fears of Germany.

Lansbury was convinced that capitalism thrived on the emotion of greed and the motive of material profit. Its resulting drive for economic expansion and domination inevitably brought nations into relationships of rivalry and fear. He therefore believed that lasting peace would only be achieved when socialism replaced competition with co-operation and rivalry with fraternity.

Lansbury foresaw war but could do nothing to prevent it. Most other socialists and most Christians considered it right to support the war. As a pacifist, he certainly did not withdraw into a corner but instead was active in several ways. First he campaigned vigorously for war dependents. The thousands of women separated from their husbands received — apart from officers' wives — meagre allowances made all the worse by inflation. Along with Sylvia Pankhurst, Minnie (the wife of Edgar Lansbury), and others he helped form the League of Rights for Soldiers' and Sailors' Wives and Relatives. With Bessie as secretary, the League made the case for proper allowances for the separated wives and, as the war progressed, for widows. Their efforts had a two-fold impact. Allowances were raised while more respectable organizations took over the role of guardian of war dependents. Meanwhile, Lansbury continued to be active locally. As Postgate records:

> His house was a centre for every sort of aid — advice on domestic problems, instruction on how to secure pension rights, prevention of evictions, assistance in reversing all sorts of personal injustices, administration of private and public relief, and very often direct financial aid.[3]

Later, after the war was over, Lansbury was to be found organizing help for sailors and soldiers as they returned to their families.

Lansbury also joined in the opposition to the introduction of conscription to the armed forces. Once again he experienced unpopularity. At meetings he was pelted with missiles and sometimes assaulted. There were even posters with captions saying, 'To the Tower with Lansbury'. He refused to be cowed and when, in 1916, conscription became law he lent his support to conscientious objectors. He attended the tribunals where persons requiring exemption had to appear. Many had their appeals rejected, were forcibly sent to the front line or brutally treated in prison. Lansbury frequently tried to intervene and, as late as 1919, he pleaded successfully with Lloyd George for the release of conscientious objectors.

Finally, he never ceased to call for an end to hostilities. In 1915 alone, the British Army suffered 300,000 casualties in France. Lansbury was appalled at the slaughter of both British and German troops. Many were the meetings he addressed pleading with Britain to take the initiative in peace negotiations. By this time, however, he was reaching far larger audiences than found in meetings. He had become editor of a newspaper with which his name will ever be associated, the *Daily Herald*.

The socialist movement had received support from a number of weekly and monthly journals, such as the *Labour Leader* and the *Clarion*, as well as from a few local papers such as the *Merthyr Pioneer* and the *Bradford Labour Echo*. But it lacked a voice amongst the national tabloids at a time when Britain had numerous daily newspapers and London alone had six evening papers. Oddly enough, the origins of the *Daily Herald* can be traced to the printers of the *Daily News*. In 1911, they went on strike for a fifty-hour week and issued a strike sheet called the *Daily Herald* which sold well at a halfpenny. It closed after the strike but it prompted some socialists, including Ben Tillett, to perceive the possibilities of a socialist newspaper. Tillett went to see his friend Lansbury at the House of Commons and, over a cup of tea, asked him to join the venture. George had some experience of journalism — although very little of editing — and realized that the chances of successfully launching a daily paper in the highly financed, highly competitive, mass circulation world of capitalist newspapers were almost nil. Yet he accepted, and on 15 April 1912 the small band of enthusiasts published their first edition. Lansbury later wrote, 'I remember taking some of my younger children for a long tram ride about East London to look at the big posters announcing our birth.'[4] They were witnessing the birth of a great newspaper to be known to generations of socialists as the *Herald*.

Charles Lapworth was the first editor and a number of people were to fill the editor's chair, with Lansbury being the most consistent. The editor, and all the journalists and compositors were crammed into one room. Funds were always in short supply. On one occasion, the paper survived only because a clergyman and his wife arrived to donate £150 out of their savings. On another, the staff had to share out the cash box for their wages and received a few pence each. Not only the editors: journalists and compositors also made sacrifices. The workers at the printers did their part. When no money was available to buy paper, the printing manager and his staff found sections of old reels and the *Herald* came out in different shapes and sizes. Once the paper's directors reluctantly decided it had to close but the staff refused to agree and published. It survived.

Initial sales reached the astonishing heights of 200,000. They were not consistently maintained, for the paper lacked the necessary funds for distributing and advertising itself. Being a socialist paper, the *Herald* was not backed by any capitalist corporations and so found it difficult to attract advertising revenue. Further, it was not even the official organ of the Labour Party, which regarded it as too extreme and which set up its own short-lived *Daily Citizen*. Opposition was almost overwhelming. Other papers sneered at its initial amateur appearance and, once war started, implied that it was in the pay of the Germans and then the Russians. Some paper manufacturers were reluctant to make supplies available. During the war, army chiefs wanted it banned and in 1919 when the *Herald* was sympathetic to the new Russian regime, the War Office did try to seize and destroy copies. At this time, the management of the

Albert Hall cancelled a *Herald* rally to celebrate its return to daily publication. Lansbury appealed to Lloyd George, who indicated that he had no powers to intervene. Members of the Electrical Trades Union then removed all fuses from the Albert Hall while buses and taxis threatened to refuse to stop there. Lloyd George decided that he could intervene, after all, and the meeting took place. It was the support of such working-class people which kept the *Herald* going. No wonder that Lansbury entitled his subsequent book *The Miracle of Fleet Street*.

The editorial policy of the *Herald* is difficult to identify during its formative years. Its Committee of Management (later Board of Directors) did not interfere with editorial decisions. The editorship was exercised in a spirit of co-operation — and sometimes conflict — with others in the one working room, with the editor having the final say. Lansbury allowed all kinds of views within a general socialist framework. Some contributions he definitely disagreed with, as when G.K. Chesterton put the case against women's suffrage. Further, he sometimes disliked the tone of some pieces which were, he said, 'mainly the good old gospel of hate. I can hate conditions with the best or worst of men, but I have never felt hatred of anybody.'[5] Within this diversity, however, some general features can be traced. Above all, the *Herald* was prepared to give a voice to a socialism which was not necessarily that of the Labour Party. In particular, Lapworth favoured articles on syndicalism. In addition, it inevitably supported strikes, such as those by seamen, dockers and transport workers. Unlike most other papers, it constantly viewed events from the perspective of working-class people. Notably, when the Titanic sunk, the *Herald* alone analysed the figures of survivors and then questioned why the safety arrangements had facilitated the escape of first-class passengers while leaving steerage passengers to drown. Next, and especially during 1912–14, the *Herald* backed votes for women. When, in May 1913, the police invaded the offices of the *Suffragette*, the *Herald*'s printers printed it. As a result its manager, Mr Drew, received a prison sentence. Its steadfast support for the women's campaign was not without some reward, for Lansbury later wrote that it:

> did a very great deal to bring women into touch with the Labour Movement. In our ranks today are many thousands of women who would never have heard of Trade Unionism and Socialism but for the suffrage agitation and the *Daily Herald*.[6]

Finally, the *Herald* took on a distinct role in war-time. During the winter of 1914–15, Lansbury went to the French trenches. He could not resist pointing out that one hospital was organized by Dr Garrett Anderson and that he 'found everybody loud in the praise of women doctors'.[7] Mostly, though, he sent the *Herald* eyewitness accounts which condemned both the madness of human slaughter and the wickedness of arms dealers who were making fortunes out of it. Consequently, the *Herald* constantly called for negotiations to end hostilities. When the *Evening News* placarded the streets with the single word 'NO' following President Woodrow Wilson's peace proposals early in 1917, the *Herald* replied with the single word 'YES'.

Overall the *Herald* stood for the rights of what Lansbury called 'the down-trodden'. It supported Irish and Indian nationalists; it ever spoke for the unemployed; it campaigned for persecuted minorities in Eastern Europe; and it highlighted the cruelties inflicted upon conscientious objectors in Britain. During 1917, when food rationing was introduced, many working-class families were going hungry. The *Herald* sent a reporter to gorge himself at the Ritz Hotel and then contrasted the luxuries of the rich with the sufferings of the poor under the headline, 'How they starve at the Ritz'. Lansbury himself said that 'we have ever been on the side of the down-trodden at home and abroad, and almost always in a minority'.[8]

The *Herald* was not just a paper. Its League of Friends used money raised through its columns to aid those in desperate need. On one occasion it fed, clothed and housed striking iron workers who marched in protest from the Midlands to London in 1912. When by-elections occurred during the war, it backed socialist candidates against the governing coalition. The League got the *Herald*'s peace proposals put forward at the Labour Party conference of 1917, where they were heavily defeated. The League, in conjunction with *Herald* staff, also organized several huge meetings, of which the most notable was one called to celebrate the Russian revolution.

In 1917, the Bolsheviks, mainly led by Lenin and Trotsky, seized power in Russia. Despite the oppressive nature of the deposed Tsarist regime, the changes were greeted with alarm by many in the West. However, sections of the Labour movement greeted it with enthusiasm, welcomed the setting up of workers' councils — soviets as they were called in Russia — and called for an end to the capitalist war. The *Herald* organized a rally at the Albert Hall both to welcome the revolution and to call for a cessation of hostilities. Twelve thousand people crowded in, standing five deep in the top gallery. They rose to sing the International and then listened to the magnificent voice of Clara Butt whose 'Give to us peace in our time, O Lord' brought tears to many eyes. Lansbury was the final speaker. It must have been one of his finest speeches for, without a microphone, his voice was heard and eagerly listened to by all. Fortunately, some parts of his speech were reported in newspapers. He welcomed the Russian revolution, saying:

> This triumph has come, friends, because for the first time that
> I know of in history — at least in modern history — soldiers,
> working-class soldiers, have refused to fire on the workers. (loud
> and continued applause) . . . we can understand that when the
> working-classes of all nations refuse to shoot down the working-
> classes of other countries, Governments won't be able to make
> wars any more. (tremendous applause).
>
>   Mr Lloyd George is head of a great Government. (Hisses).
> Comrades, don't let us hoot anyone here. We disagree about lots
> of things, but we are all wanting to celebrate a giant proletarian
> revolt: we don't want to bother our heads about hooting anyone.
> After all, he is the head of our Government. I believe this —
> that if he and his colleagues would whole-heartedly back the
> programme sent out by the Revolutionary Labour Party of
> Russia, we could get an International that would be a bulwark
> for the future freedom of the whole of the human race. Now we
> English people have to clean our own door-step. I stood here just
> about three years ago: almost where Williams is sitting sat James
> Connolly. (Applause). He and his murdered colleagues of a year
> ago were just too soon, that is all; and, friends, we British people
> have got to clear that Irish question up, because until we do it
> is not for us to celebrate other people's triumphs over reaction.
> Further, there are to-night hundreds of young men in gaol; there
> are to-night thousands of young men in India who are there in
> gaol. The people of India, the people of Ireland, the people of
> Ceylon, ask that we who claim to be the leaders in democracy
> in the world shall put our principles into practice at home. Now
> most of us here, every man and every woman who is gathered in
> this hall, have some sort of feeling and love and care for other
> men and women, and I think the one great outstanding thing
> to realise in regard to Russia and the working-class movement

is just this, that if this great human race is to work out its
salvation, it is by men and women like you and me doing it.
You have to get rid of the idea that someone else can emancipate
you, someone else can save you. We here in Britain — what is the
thing that keeps us backward? It is our jealousies, our fears, and
anxiety to find out where we disagree instead of where we agree.
I want to see this Russian movement impelling you and me to
catch their spirit, their enthusiasm, and be ready to suffer, and
if needs be to die, for our faith. Men and women, the hardest
thing is to live for our faith, and that is what you and I have got
to do. Here and there in our country there are things that want
clearing up. Some of them I just now mentioned. But do not
go home without realising that in British prisons, for religious,
for political offences, some of the best of the young men of this
country are dying. Do not forget that in Russia they have thrown
open the prisons. (Applause.) Do not forget in Russia they have
put down police spies.

'To the young men — if there are any here; to the young
women — there are many here — I want to say this: you
are celebrating to-night a tremendous thing. It is fine to cheer
these other people, fine to feel you can sing about them, talk
about them; a finer thing still is to emulate and follow their
example. (Loud and prolonged applause.) It is men and women
of goodwill, irrespective of race, who will redeem the world. You
men and women gathered here in such magnificent numbers will
go out with the words of the song you have sung ringing in your
ears, and remember always the duty laid upon each of you. 'Quit
you like men, be strong'.[9]

Lansbury sat down to ringing applause. Ten years later he wrote,
'It seemed as if all the long pent-up feelings of horror and shame
of war and intense longing for peace were at last let loose . . .
I reckon the meeting as one of the chief of the many services
rendered to the cause of peace and Socialism by the *Herald*'.[10]
He was too modest to add that the size of the crowd was partly
due to his own drawing power. Despite being derided by the press
for his pacifism, his peace proposals and his support for the Russian
revolution, Lansbury had a place in the hearts of many citizens.
That place was due to the respect he had won in their eyes as a
man of integrity and honesty, as one steadfast in his loyalty to the
oppressed, and as a socialist who lived out his principles.

During the war, a shortage of paper forced the *Herald* into being a weekly publication. Once peace was established, Lansbury raised cash from trade unions, co-operative societies and from individuals, including the unlikely and modest socialist, Countess De La Warr. The paper was re-launched as a daily on 31 March 1919, and its first edition declared:

> We shall work increasingly for a revolution, peaceful but complete, which shall destroy the present system of competition and . . . replace it by the rule of co-operation.

By the 1920s, its paid circulation was 329,869 and its influence such that the government smeared it by suggesting that it was financed by Soviet cash. The *Herald* promptly printed a complete list of donors to disprove the charge. Later, Francis Meynell, a director of the paper, did obtain Russian money offered without any conditions. Moreover, Edgar Lansbury played some part in the negotiations. Lansbury put a front-page question, 'Shall we accept £75,000 of Russian money?' and eventually decided against. But some damage had been done and Meynell resigned.

The *Herald* desperately needed that money. The cost of paper was soaring so, as Lansbury explained, 'The more copies we sold, the more money we lost.'[11] Many papers were depending on their advertising revenue, but private firms were mainly unwilling to advertise in a paper which advocated public ownership of the likes of them. The price of the *Herald* had to be raised to twopence, twice that of its rivals. Even so, at a time of great unemployment, it still maintained a circulation of 200,000, an achievement which Lord Northcliffe of the *Daily Mail* called 'a miracle'.

Nonetheless, the financial problems seemed insuperable. The directors of the *Herald* refused bids from commercial publishers who wanted ownership of a mass-circulation paper which reached working-class people. Instead they turned to the Labour Party and the TUC which, in 1923, took over the shares of the Victoria House Printing Company and so assumed control of the paper. The take-over did not receive universal backing, for some Labour figures considered the paper would always be a financial liability. Among those who backed the take-over were a number who wanted to replace Lansbury by an editor more in line with official Labour policies. The experienced Hamilton Fyfe became editor, and Lansbury's contribution was recognized by appointing him as general manager. However, he did not approve of a number of editorial changes which followed. As McKibbon sharply commented, 'It was Lansbury more than anyone else who forced the *Herald* on a reluctant Labour movement . . . Yet he resented it when his editorial policy was criticised . . .'[12]

Lansbury left the *Herald* altogether in 1925 and then unwisely allowed some colleagues to persuade him to lend his name to a new weekly called *Lansbury's Labour Weekly*. Virtually no advertisers would touch it and, after a promising start, it was amalgamated with another journal in 1927. But Lansbury's heart was really in the *Herald* and he wrote, at this time:

> The Labour movement has one daily paper . . . we should all
> consider it a sacred duty not only to keep it going, but to assist
> in making it the biggest and most powerful weapon for Socialism
> in the world.[13]

In 1927, the Labour Party could not meet its financial share and the TUC took over full control. But the cash problems remained and in 1929 the TUC, leaning heavily on the negotiating skills of Ernie Bevin, went into partnership with Odhams Press. Odhams provided the business oversight but four directors appointed by the TUC shaped the political flavour. Lansbury must have been delighted when its circulation subsequently rose to almost two million even though he regretted that the success depended partially on giving less coverage to politics and more to sport, bathing beauties and free gifts. As Geoffrey Goodman, himself a renowned *Herald* journalist, put it, 'Lansbury's inspiration was essential for the *Herald* up till the mid-1920s', but his ideas were '. . . simply not applicable to the later period of intense commercial competition among the national newspapers'.[14] The paper outlived Lansbury and survived until 1964, when the TUC sold its shares to the International Publishing Corporation which subsequently changed the *Herald* into the *Sun*, which became anything but a socialist paper. Thus Lansbury saw the *Herald* grow from little more than a broadsheet to a mass circulation paper.

The *Herald* was by no means the only socialist publication in this period. The Fabian intellectuals, as Cole makes clear, considered that it 'could hardly be called a serious journal' . . . 'and went on to found the *New Statesman*.[15] It was not even the official voice of the Labour Party and Ramsay MacDonald, who had become leader of the party, frequently complained that it failed to give enough coverage to official policy and that it fed the popular prejudice that Labour was dominated by communists. Unintellectual and unofficial notwithstanding, the *Herald* was important in expressing, for working-class people, a view that was not found in other dailies. For instance, after the end of the war, the *Herald* stood almost alone in not demanding vengeance against Germany and in foreseeing that the terms of the Treaty of Versailles with its annexation of German colonies and imposition of enormous reparations would lead to another war. It was the *Herald* which condemned the massacre of Indians by British troops in Amritsar in 1919, which spoke against the imprisonment of Mahatma Ghandi in 1922, and which supported the latter's tactics of non-violence and his goal of self-government. At home, during the General Strike of 1926, when the *Star*, the *Daily News* and the *Daily Mail* were attacking strikers for undermining the economic life of the nation, it was the *Herald* which put the strikers' case by showing how their incomes had been slashed in real terms. Thus the traditional historian, Maurice Cowling, who has hardly a good word to say about Lansbury, admits that the *Herald* provided a 'fundamental challenge' to the existing establishment.[16] Another distinguished historian, and one with much more positive views of Lansbury, A.J.P. Taylor, concludes that the *Herald* 'broke the old monopoly of established opinion and bore witness that the people of England were not all thinking as their rulers thought they should'.[17]

The *Herald*'s view was not just different, not just challenging: it was socialist. Harry McShane, an outstanding working-class leader in Scotland, wrote that 'from 1912 the paper appeared regularly. I got the paper every morning and read it avidly.'[18] In April 1918, Lansbury's old socialist friend, W. Dingwall, wrote to him from Port Glasgow that the *Herald* was 'now a part of my life'. Although he could no longer afford butter, he refused to give up the *Herald*. For thousands of working-class people, it became their daily means of interpreting events in a socialist way and a means of encouraging them in their socialist beliefs.

In accounts of this period, Lansbury's name is always linked with the *Herald*. Yet he did not found it. He was not the sole editor and others took over when he was abroad or ill. In his books, Lansbury was insistent that the other editors — Charles Lapworth, Rowland Keeney, Sheridan Jones, W.H. Seed — be given credit. In particular, he praised the poet Gerald Gould who was associate editor for a number of years. While visiting France during the war, Gerald tricked the teetotal Lansbury into taking brandy in his coffee by saying it was a French syrup. He only enlightened Lansbury when the latter liked it so much that he was requesting it every day. Lansbury appreciated the joke and he appreciated Gould's contribution to the *Herald*.

Eager as Lansbury was to praise the part of others, there is little doubt that his was the main influence. As editor, he succeeded in drawing in a wide range of notable contributors. The Catholic Hilaire Belloc, the Anglican G.K. Chesterton, the guild socialist G.D.H. Cole, the novelist E.M. Forster, the cartoonist Will Dyson, all were regular contributors. Periodic pieces came from Siegfried Sassoon, Havelock Ellis, Alec Waugh, Rebecca West, Rose Macaulay, Aldous Huxley and Robert Graves. Not all were socialists. Some wrote without taking a fee. All seemed to admire the *Herald*. Lansbury gave them, and lesser names, guidance and encouragement. Sometimes he expressed concern about articles which made savage, personal attacks on opponents and he urged restraint. Interestingly, Langdon Everard, who became a notable journalist, wrote a letter in April 1916, thanking Lansbury for his advice and saying that 'it looks as though the milk of human kindness has taken the place of vitriol and this I owe to you'.

As a prolific writer himself, Lansbury put a Christian stamp upon the *Herald*. He recalled:

> As I was editor we found it very easy to make our stand against all war a very definite one on Christian lines. My correspondence during the war years and since convinces me that much more than many churches or clergy, the *Herald* helped people to preserve their faith in religion.[19]

One article entitled 'Christ's call to peace' in 1918 evoked a large response. Thus a Charles Horner wrote to thank Lansbury and contrasted his call for forgiveness with that of a well known clergyman, the Rev. J.B. Meyer, who had written to the *Daily News* that he would not meet enemy Christians till they showed signs of repentance. Lansbury inserted a Christian slant on such issues as war and peace, wealth and poverty, private and public ownership, and so won readers who might have been Christians but not socialists to the *Herald*.

Above all, Lansbury kept the *Herald* alive. To this end, he had to design a paper which appealed to working-class readers. As well as lively political comment, it contained popular news, literary items, sports reports and two features which he included with some reluctance, betting tips and the annual honours list. In addition, Lansbury had to seek supplies of printing paper, which he did with success; find extra sources of funding, which he did with moderate success; and seek advertising revenue, with which he had little success. The *Herald* never possessed financial security yet somehow Lansbury and his colleagues enabled it to survive until it was taken over by the TUC. He thus confounded Bernard Shaw, who once wrote him a postcard on which he scribbled, 'Neither you nor anybody else can keep a daily Labour paper going.' Lansbury, more than any other person, established the *Herald* not just as a great national paper but as the daily voice of British socialism.

Michael Foot, like Lansbury, became a journalist, editor, MP and leader of the Labour Party. He knew Lansbury and in an interview had this to say:

> One of the best achievements in socialist journalism has been what the *Herald* did after the 1918 war. It played a leading part in changing the way people thought about war and its consequences and a leading part in stopping British intervention in Russia. The Labour Party came into its full strength between 1918–29 and Lansbury played a foremost part in all that for he was one of the very best propagandists in the whole field. Lansbury was a very fine journalist. When in charge of the *Daily Herald* he was a fine editor. He got together a magnificent lot of people writing for him. Lansbury's part in the post 1918 *Herald* has not been given sufficient credit. He ran the best Labour newspaper there has ever been in this country.

If Lansbury had established the *Herald* with extensive financial backing and from a background of editorial experience, it would have been a remarkable achievement. Astonishingly, he laid the foundations of a great newspaper while always short of funds, with little previous experience and in the face of constant opposition from commercial interests.

Lansbury's association with the *Herald* did much to increase his standing as a national figure. In wartime, the *Herald* was the most widely read anti-war publication and, as Postgate observed, it gave Lansbury 'a national eminence which he had not had before'.[20] As editor of the *Herald*, Lansbury obtained access to leading statesmen as he interviewed them about war and peace. He made an impression upon President Woodrow Wilson, who took a leading role in the negotiations which followed the end of the war. Wilson had listened to Lansbury's arguments that the peace terms should not be so harsh as to leave Germany with a bitterness that would sow the seeds of future war. When the treaty was signed, and knowing that Lansbury would be disappointed, the President wrote him a personal letter explaining, 'I have done what I found it absolutely necessary to do and not what I wanted to do.' Not least, through the *Herald* Lansbury became known to every section of the Labour movement in Britain and so paved the way for a possible resumption of a parliamentary career which seemed to have ended in 1912.

As the war came to a close, Lansbury and other Labour candidates had high hopes of electoral success. The coalition government had taken control of coal mines, railways and shipping; it had imposed rent controls on certain dwellings; and it had established a wages board to ensure minimum wages for agricultural labourers. Labour supporters believed that the success of these collectivist measures would convince the public that socialist practices were also needed in peacetime. Moreover, Henderson had demonstrated that a working-class Labour MP could be a capable cabinet minister. Outside of parliament, Henderson had been prominent in reorganizing the Labour Party's structure so that in 1918 it adopted a new constitution which replaced its loose federation by constituency branches and individual membership. In addition, the Representation of the People Act of 1918 had extended the electorate to include virtually all men aged over twenty-one and all women aged over thirty (reduced to twenty-one in 1928).

Labour left the coalition to fight the 1918 general election. Its hopes were not fulfilled. Only a quarter of the armed forces were able to vote, and Lloyd George capitalized on his image as a war leader. The coalition of Conservatives and Lloyd George Liberals won 478 seats, Labour 59 and other Liberals 26. The split within the Liberal ranks, which foretold its end as a major political party, meant that Labour became the official opposition. But, with its leading figures of Henderson, MacDonald and Snowden all losing their seats, the election was not a Labour Party success. Lansbury again contested Bow and Bromley. Rose Rosamund —

later a Labour mayor — recalled that she and other children held Lansbury's hand and followed him around the streets. She wrote that he carried a 'very large furry black cat with him and we all used to sing Vote, Vote, Vote for Mr Lansbury'.[21] But children do not vote and Lansbury lost to the Conservatives by 942 votes.

Out of parliament, Lansbury decided to visit Russia. The British government and press were painting the new leaders in Russia as a band of bloodthirsty barbarians who had brought the country to its knees. Lansbury wanted to see for himself. The Poplar Borough Council gave him leave, for he was mayor at the time, and by roundabout and perilous routes he made his way to Moscow and then toured the whole country visiting factories, farms, hospitals, churches and prisons and talking to officials, soldiers, priests, labourers and peasants.

He was the first British editor to visit the new Russia and his reports were soon appearing in the *Herald*. These flatly contradicted the stories in other papers that all ports, churches and most factories were closed. He explained that workers were involved in running industries, that Christians were worshipping and that most citizens welcomed the overthrow of the Tsarist regime. He also acknowledged that 'poverty and want were in evidence everywhere' but added that much of the blame for food shortages had to be laid at the door of the allies who were blockading Russian ports.[22] Lansbury returned to Britain to crowds awaiting him at the station and a tumultuous meeting at the Albert Hall where he proclaimed the virtues of the socialist revolution.

In 1926, accompanied by Bessie, Lansbury went to Russia again. They were met and guided around by their youngest daughter, Violet. Violet had become a communist and had worked as a typist at the Russian Trade Delegation in London. She moved to Russia in 1925 and later married Igor Reussner. In a book, describing her years in Russia, Violet tells how she was delegated to meet her parents. She waited for their ship and wrote that:

There they were on the lower deck, waving their handkerchiefs and smiling, surrounded, as father always seemed to be, by ordinary, simple folk, members of the crew . . . As we approached the waiting car, father turned to the chauffeur with his usual Cockney 'Whatch'er comrade', and the astonished chauffeur, seeing his cheerful countenance, grinned broadly in greeting, though he did not understand the words.[23]

Bessie took to Russia immediately. She spent hours in the museums and art galleries, where George eventually became bored and tired. She displayed a grasp of economics which surprised Violet. These were precious times for mother and daughter and Violet recorded:

> During these short periods, when alone with my mother, I was perhaps happier than at any other time. For one thing, being the youngest daughter of a large family, I had never really known my mother or thought of her personal feelings. I had merely looked upon her as somebody in authority . . . who perpetually pulled me up for dirty shoes, no gloves, and my habit of never wearing a hat. There in Moscow I saw her differently. She was calm and happy, freed from the endless burden of running a house. She put all her freed energy into watching, trying to understand, shedding her sweetness and charm on all and sundry. And she never forgot for one moment that everything she was enjoying had been built up by working hands.[24]

As for George, Violet admitted:

> As usual I found father's heartiness a little embarrassing. Neither did my mother ever really get used to his 'hail-fellow-well-met' attitude to people in general. Father always had a way of treating everybody as though they were just another bit of his family; he was always without restraint and nothing could ever hold back his natural exuberance.[25]

George's outgoing friendliness and willingness to see good did not prevent him from observing, 'There was still poverty and unemployment and still many thousands of destitute, homeless children.'[26] However, he was convinced that the changes in housing, transport and work conditions were a great improvement for most citizens compared with their previous lot as serfs and slaves. He remained convinced that it was a good thing: 'This Russian Revolution is the greatest human event in my lifetime.'[27] Bessie was even more convinced. She had frequently given shelter to refugees from Russia and knew all about their previous persecutions and sufferings. From henceforth she became a quiet but firm supporter of the new regime.

Lansbury's reports in the *Herald* and his book, *What I Saw In Russia*, published in 1920, were heavily criticized yet had a profound effect. As one of the few British eyewitnesses in Russia, he was able to counter much of the anti-revolutionary propaganda in other papers. He stimulated greater pro-Russian feeling, which surfaced strongly in 1919 and 1920 when the British government seemed poised to use force to intervene in Russia in order to restore the old regime. The Labour Party sent to Russia an official delegation whose observations have been fully recorded by one of its members, Margaret Bondfield, and which concluded that 'we found nothing in Russia to justify the policy of making war upon her'.[28] Feeling within the Labour movement became so strong that it set up a Council of Action to oppose any war of intervention, the TUC threatened a general strike, and dockers refused to load munitions destined for Polish troops who were fighting the Russians. Eventually, Lloyd George backed down and Postgate declared, 'There was no British war on Russia; a major part of government policy had been altered, forcibly, by the intervention of another power. That other power was the organised working class of its own country.'[29] Postgate exaggerates, for there were other voices counselling Lloyd George against what would have been an ill-fated intervention in Eastern Europe. But, beyond doubt, the socialist pressure was a major factor and that pressure had been stimulated by Lansbury's writings about Russia. Thus the official *Encyclopaedia of the Labour Movement* — which criticized some of Lansbury's left-wing leanings — paid tribute to his 'magnificent work in leading the Opposition against Allied intervention in Russia, in meeting the very real danger of the involving of this country in a Polish-Russian War, and in assisting the victims of the terrible famine in Russia'.[30]

Lansbury's reports on Russia impressed and rallied support from many Labour sympathizers. Simultaneously, they provoked furious reactions from Conservative sources which accused him of viewing that country through rose-tinted spectacles, a criticism which was to increase in later years when Stalinism took a grip on Russian politics. The *Evening Standard* claimed that he had been duped by Soviet officials and that he was 'constitutionally incapable of knowing . . . incapable of learning'. It continued, in its edition of 3 April 1920, to call him 'the self-elected Messiah of British Bolshevism', and made much of the pacifist Lansbury's apparent countenance of the violence leading to the Russian revolution. At the opposite end of the political spectrum, Sylvia Pankhurst mocked him for using militant language in support of the Russian revolution yet refusing to leave the Labour Party to join the British Communist Party when it was formed in 1920.

Certainly, Lansbury did exaggerate the beneficial effects of the revolution and he failed to perceive that it was moving towards the dictatorship and terrors of Stalin. However, he did not gloss over all the deficiencies. He described the hunger, the beggars, the unemployment. He recorded the 'rigid discipline, suppression of opinions, abolition of freedom of public debate and meeting', while adding that such freedoms had not existed in pre-revolutionary Russia and that their present imposition occurred at a time when the revolutionary government was facing civil war within and threats from other countries without.[31]

Further, Lansbury always perceived and regretted the undemocratic nature of what developed in Russia (or the Soviet as it was increasingly called). Beatrice and Sydney Webb became devotees and, in the 1930s, Beatrice proudly proclaimed 'fallen in love with Soviet Communism'.[32] By contrast, in 1924 Lansbury supported the Labour Party's decision not to admit communists to membership because he believed, unlike them, that the road to British socialism was via peaceful and democratic means. He wrote, 'The Labour Party road may seem a longer way round than was adopted by our Russian comrades. All the same, it is our only way and is more safe, more enduring, than any the world has yet known.'[33]

Lansbury's attitude to the Russian revolution was complicated but consistent. He welcomed it because it overthrew a cruel, oppressive and undemocratic regime. He understood that radical change in Russia could not have been achieved by the ballot box. He rejoiced that the new system gave more power and opportunities to working-class people and he believed that it would eventually evolve into a fully democratic and socialist society. Yet Lansbury never advocated violence and never called for any kind of government except an elected one. He remained convinced that, in Britain, socialism could and would be achieved by peaceful and democratic avenues. He wrote:

On no occasion have we supported the Bolshevik theory of Government. On the contrary, we have always declared ourselves against dictatorship . . . But we claimed for Soviet Russia the right to try out an experiment which at least gave the promise of freedom from the curse of Tsardom and capitalism.'[34]

Lansbury's trips to Russia did open his eyes to the limitations and dangers of communist theory and practice. Yet he returned both cheered and encouraged. He saw collective rather than private control of the means of production. His belief that the elected representatives of workers could manage factories was confirmed. Even more, he felt strengthened by meetings with revolutionary figures. In moving words, he described his visit to a leading official, Krassin:

> Often when I hear ignorant Members of Parliament and ministers of religion denouncing the horrors of Bolshevism I see a vision of my friend and comrade Krassin, pale and wan, sitting at a desk in a room that was like an ice-well. The day was one of the coldest I experienced and Krassin, though a leading minister of the Soviet, was suffering all the ills which poverty and want of food brings, bearing on his face all the marks of privation and starvation. The same day I visited two children's homes and saw 200 children at each home sit down to a dinner of good, wholesome soup, boiled chicken, and vegetables. I wonder how many of us, labour leaders and others, myelf included, ever suffered any shortage of food and firing during a strike or lock-out, when our comrades have been starving? I wonder more how many cabinet ministers during the war went short while poor children got food?[35]

Lansbury also had a long interview with Lenin in which they disagreed over the existence of God, the use of violence and the part of propaganda. When Lansbury took up the restraints placed on the press and public meetings in Russia, Lenin replied that Britain had suppressed similar freedoms in Ireland and India. But it was not Lenin's views on politics which most impressed Lansbury. Rather it was the kind of life he led. Lansbury noted that Lenin looked half-starved yet remained cheerful. He had just escaped an assassination attempt yet met Lansbury without any guards. He dressed like an artisan and worked in a plain room. Lansbury declared that Lenin:

> was loved as no other statesman was ever loved, not merely because he was leader and chief inspirer of the Revolution, but because his daily life, his attitude towards his fellow men never changed.[36]

Lansbury believed that socialism was about changing the structures of society, changing the distribution of income, wealth and power. He also believed that it was about principles lived out in the lives of individuals. He admired Lenin as a socialist who tried to live according to his principles. The effect on Lansbury was to encourage him in his efforts to practise a socialist way of life.

Lenin was an atheist. This fact did not prevent Lansbury from liking and admiring him. Nor did it prevent him from talking to Lenin about Christianity. For Christianity was integral to Lansbury's life and hence to his socialism. His religious foundations featured most strongly in a book which he wrote in 1917 entitled *Your Part in Poverty*. In a preface, the Bishop of Winchester, while distancing himself from Lansbury's politics, wrote that he wanted 'to prevent Churchmanship from being bound up with Toryism'.[37] Lansbury's book certainly avoided that for it powerfully argued that Conservative values and capitalist systems led to a poverty and suffering which were contrary to God's intentions and which could only be fully countered by socialism. The book is one of Lansbury's best, direct in style, full of personal experience yet applicable to all of society. It provided his first full account of his principles and beliefs.

Lansbury painted a vivid picture of poverty and wealth. Both, he declared, were evils: poverty because it created extreme anxieties, blighted intellectual and physical growth, and crushed families; wealth because it made its owners selfish and greedy. But why were income and wealth so unevenly distributed? Lansbury pointed the finger at the continuing divisions of social class. He poured scorn on 'press talk about the breakdown of class distinctions' and contrasted the power, opulence and lifestyles of the owners of capital with the weakness and misery of the low-paid and unemployed.[38] The former used their ownership to oppress the producers, the working class, not just with low wages but also with unhealthy work conditions and the threat of unemployment.

Charity, Lansbury maintained, was not the answer for the victims of capitalism. He appreciated those middle-class women from good schools and privileged backgrounds who visited and conveyed services to poor people. But they were too geographically and socially removed from those they visited. How, Lansbury asked, can such a woman 'possibly be a workmate in the full sense unless she is actually living on the same wage?'[39] Further, he explained, voluntary effort of this kind only made life a little easier for a few people; it did not reduce the income differences between them and the affluent.

The solution, in Lansbury's view, was the social ownership of land, coal, and other industries. Such collective ownership would both eliminate the evil of competition and also allow rewards to be more evenly distributed. Lansbury was convinced that such a change of ownership would happen only when a working-class party achieved political power and appointed working-class leaders who really understood and represented their problems and needs.

Middle-class citizens who sympathized with the aims of socialism nevertheless had a part to play. Interestingly, Lansbury addressed much of his book to them and urged 'every man and woman who wants to change things to get into the working-class movement'.[40]

However, Lansbury perceived that often middle-class socialists entered the movement in order to dominate it and so actually operated to perpetuate the inferior position of working-class members. Instead of wanting to be leaders, they should be ready to be servants who enabled others to take on positions of responsibility. He stated:

> They should join in order to be part of it [the movement] . . .
> keeping steadily in mind the fact that *true* democracy means
> people thinking and doing things for themselves.[41]

The questions that then arose were what would motivate the affluent to sacrifice their interests for the poor and what would move working-class people to participate more fully in political activity? At this juncture, Lansbury's Christianity becomes crucial. He believed that the affluent and powerful needed to be convicted of their sins which had tolerated the social sufferings of others. He believed that working-class people needed to be possessed by the Christian vision of social justice and so stimulated to work ceaselessly for a new order. If both middle and working classes were filled with Christian love for their neighbour then they would have the common objective of a classless nation where the abundance of God's world would be shared by all.

Thus, in *Your Part in Poverty*, in articles and speeches, George Lansbury constantly referred to Christianity and argued that applied Christianity on earth would lead to a different kind of state — a socialist state. His efforts provoked many responses from Christians. Some welcomed his insistence that a true interpretation of Christianity should be expressed in socialist practice. Some opposed him on the grounds that it was a Christian duty to uphold those in authority which, in Britain, meant supporting the capitalist system and the existing class structure. Some argued that politics and Christianity should be kept apart. Some were just pleased that a leading politician and editor was prepared to identify himself with the cause of Christ. One outcome of this public debate about Lansbury's Christianity was many invitations to speak at churches. For example, early in 1918 he spoke at the St Martin-in-the-Fields Guild of Fellowship and soon after at the anniversary service at the East India Road Presbyterian Church. He was also drawn into a number of church organizations. The Church Socialist League had dwindled but Lansbury became a member of the London Diocesan Conference and the House of Laymen, which were influential bodies in Anglican circles. Not least, Lansbury came into contact with many Christians, some of whom became his supporters and friends. One was George Dempster, the superintendent of The Sailor's Palace in Commercial Road. An evangelical, who later wrote the widely read *Finding Men for Christ*, Dempster was not politically active but in 1918 he wrote to Lansbury to express his regret that George had been defeated in the general election. Another was William Lax, the Methodist minister who became known as 'Lax of Poplar'. Like Lansbury he served as mayor of Poplar, although he was a Liberal not a socialist. Despite being in a different political camp, Lax admired and respected his fellow Christian and wrote:

> George Lansbury is the patron saint of Poplar . . . If it was possible for a city or a borough to take on human shape or qualities, Poplar would be what you know George Lansbury to be. They love each other. [42]

Lax asked what were the sources of Lansbury's power and then supplied a three-fold answer: First, 'his passion for social righteousness'; second, 'a rich supply of the milk of human kindness;' third, 'religion . . . God, conscience and religion are the beginning and end of things for him, and it is from that source that he derives his strength and courage'. [43]

As Lax indicated, Lansbury felt completely at home in the East End. In August 1916, he and Bessie and the children moved to 39

Bow Road, which was to be both their home for the rest of their lives and the hub of George's local government activities.

References

[1]   G. Lansbury, *These Things Shall Be*, Swarthmore Press, 1920, p. 28.

[2]   G. Lansbury, *My England*, Selwyn and Blount, 1934, p. 191.

[3]   R. Postgate, *The Life of George Lansbury*, Longmans, Green & Co., 1951, p. 154.

[4]   G. Lansbury, *The Miracle of Fleet Street*, Victoria House and Labour Publishing Co., 1925, p. 10.

[5]   Ibid., pp. 33–34.

[6]   Ibid., pp. 76–77.

[7]   G. Lansbury, *My Life*, Constable, 1928, p. 184.

[8]   Lansbury, *Miracle of Fleet Street*, p. 22.

[9]   Cited in Postgate, *Life of George Lansbury*, pp. 167–68.

[10]   Lansbury, *My Life*, pp. 186–87.

[11]   Cited in S. Koss, *The Rise and Fall of the Political Press in Britain*, vol. 2, Hamish Hamilton, 1984, p. 6.

[12]   R. McKibbon, *The Evolution of the Labour Party, 1910–1924*, Oxford University Press, 1974, p. 233.

[13]   Lansbury, *My Life*, p. 195.

[14]   G. Goodman, letter to the author.

[15]   M. Cole, *Beatrice Webb*, Longmans, Green & Co., 2nd edition, 1946, p. 124.

[16]   M. Cowling, *The Impact of Labour 1920–1924*, Cambridge University Press, 1971, p. 35.

[17]   A.J.P. Taylor, *English History 1914–1945*, Penguin Books, reprinted 1987, p. 191.

[18]   H. McShane and J. Smith, *No Mean Fighter*, Pluto Press, 1978, p. 50.

[19]   Lansbury, *My Life*, p. 185.

[20]   Postgate, *Life of George Lansbury*, p. 155.

[21]   Mrs R. Rosamund, personal communication to author.

[22]   Lansbury, *My Life*, p. 233.

[23]   V. Lansbury, *An Englishwoman in the USSR*, Putman, 1940, p. 123.

24 Ibid., p. 131.

25 Ibid., p. 123.

26 Lansbury, *My Life*, p. 259.

27 Ibid., p. 261.

28 M. Bondfield, *A Life's Work*, Hutchinson & Co., 1948, p. 234.

29 Postgate, *Life of George Lansbury*, p. 209.

30 H. Lees-Smith (ed.), *Encyclopaedia of the Labour Movement*, vol. 2, Caxton Publishing Co., 1924, p. 199.

31 Lansbury, *My Life*, p. 229.

32 Cited by M. Cole, *Beatrice Webb*, p. 173.

33 Lansbury, *My Life*, p. 264.

34 Lansbury, *Miracle of Fleet Street*, p. 39.

35 Lansbury, *My Life*, pp. 229–30.

36 Ibid., p. 245.

37 G. Lansbury, *Your Part in Poverty*, The Herald, 1917, pp. 12–13.

38 Ibid., pp. 15–16.

39 Ibid., p. 18.

40 Ibid., p. 108.

41 Ibid., p. 109.

42 W. Lax, *Lax His Book*, The Epworth Press, 1937, p. 291.

43 Ibid, pp. 292–93.

6

PRISON AND POPLARISM

In September 1921, the British newspapers gave prominence to one story — Lansbury was in Brixton prison. Not just him but also most of his fellow Labour councillors from the Poplar borough council. Poplar had become the centre of a struggle which gave rise to a new political term — Poplarism. The meaning of 'Poplarism' depended on the values of the people who used it. To some it meant Labour Guardians and councillors needlessly spending public money on luxuries for the undeserving poor. To others, it meant elected working-class representatives using the system to protect citizens from the worst effects of poverty. A.J.P. Taylor stated, 'Poplarism became the name for any defiance by local (Labour) councils of the central government.'[1]

Poplar, as one of the most poverty-stricken boroughs in London, attracted the attention of Beatrice and Sydney Webb in 1914.[2] Unemployment was common among its population of 160,000. The borough lacked heavy industry but contained many small factories, workshops and sweatshops. Consequently, even those citizens in jobs tended to be unskilled, unorganized and badly paid. From 1914, the war took many men and women out of unemployment. However, at its close, returning soldiers and sailors found anything but a land 'fit for heroes'. After a short-lived post-war boom, unemployment began to rise. The needy might be dealt with by three bodies. Ex-servicemen and their dependants often qualified for allowances from the new Ministry of Pensions which had none of the stigma of the Poor Law. The dependants of officers received about double that of other ranks. In Poplar, the wives and children were predominantly from the other ranks and their allowances were barely sufficient to take them out of poverty. Some other workers had claim to national insurance schemes whose coverage had been extended in 1920. Unfortunately, payments were at a low level and the scheme was not designed to deal with long-term unemployment. For those without other means of support, there remained the Poor Law. All the inhabitants suffered further from inflation and rising prices. Many also experienced the dampness, inadequate sanitation and overcrowding frequently found in the dwellings which they rented from private landlords. Father St John Groser, who started his ministry in Poplar in 1922, described parents bravely struggling to survive in accommodation in which a density of two persons per room was common and six a room not unknown.[3] Not surprisingly, the socially depriving conditions had an adverse effect on children. The gallant school teacher Clara Grant, who spent a lifetime working and living in the East End, identified the outcomes for children: unfulfilled potential at school; vulnerability to illnesses and diseases of all kinds, including TB; and a child death rate much higher than in most other local authority areas.[4]

Much of the reponsibility for the relief of destitution and the provision of services rested with the Board of Guardians and the borough council. For the first time, the Labour Party was in full control for, in the elections of 1919, it gained fifteen out of twenty-four of the Guardian places and thirty-nine out of forty-two seats of the borough council. Lansbury became Poplar's first Labour mayor. Predominantly working class, the Guardians and councillors (and some individuals were both Guardians and councillors) determined to improve conditions. The Royal Commission of Housing of 1917 had stated that 'most of the troubles we have been investigating are due to the failure of private enterprise to provide and maintain the necessary houses, sufficient in quantity and quality'.[5] Socialists saw the answer as councils building for people not profit. Within two months of becoming mayor, Lansbury cut the first piece of turf at the site of a council housing scheme on the Isle of Dogs and further schemes became a feature of the borough's work. Within two years, Poplar, along with other Labour councils, established a four pounds-a-week minimum wage for its employees, including equal pay for women.

The councillors were particularly concerned about the effect on poor families of the high prices and shortage of milk and coal. On 23 December 1919, Lansbury led a deputation of London councillors to the prime minister, Lloyd George. Lansbury explained that not only were some families going short of milk and fuel but that also boroughs such as Poplar could hardly fulfil their duties to supply milk to young children and expectant and nursing mothers. When the prime minister replied that the free market system of demand and supply would eventually adjust prices so as to be in reach of all, a councillor retorted that most milk supplies in East London were controlled by one large combine which set its own prices. The argument became so heated that Lloyd George warned the councillors to be civil or to get out. The meeting achieved little but it did contain two ingredients which were to dominate the politics of councils like Poplar. Their rateable values did not generate sufficient income to run adequate services for their needy populations. This disparity was leading them into conflict with central bodies.

In 1920, the National Unemployed Workers' Movement (NUWM) was formed by unemployed persons. One of its main leaders, the communist Wal Hannington, later recorded an account of their marches and the pressure they put on bodies responsible for administering relief.[6] Lansbury welcomed such pressure and, in the *Herald*, encouraged the workless to approach Guardians for out-relief — and out-relief set at adequate levels. The Poplar Guardians then found themselves facing large crowds outside their office demanding relief. Lansbury was neither afraid nor resentful. He hated poverty. He saw daily ill-nourished children and distraught parents who had parted with children they could not afford to feed and clothe. He preferred poor people to be angry rather than apathetic.

Subject to pressure of this kind, a number of Boards of Guardians asked advice of the Ministry of Health, now the central government department responsible for the Poor Law. Should they extend out-relief or receive more families into what were still known as the workhouses? The ministry felt that to allow ex-servicemen, as many of the unemployed and destitute were, to enter the workhouses would fuel public discontent. It therefore cited Article 12 of the Relief Regulation Order of 1912 which permitted out-door relief, under certain conditions, even to those whose existing insurance benefits were too low. The green light was lit and the Poplar Guardians in particular began to administer widespread out-relief.

In a period of six months, Poplar's expenditure on out-relief doubled to £80,000. Local expenditure had to come from local rates. The problem was that Poplar was a poor borough. Postgate explains that Poplar had a rateable value of only £947,109 so that a penny rate produced £3,647. By contrast, Westminster, with far fewer poor residents, had a rateable value of £7,913,538 which produced £31,719.[7] To finance more out-relief, Poplar would have had to increase its rates once more. This step would not only have provoked the fierce opposition of the Municipal Alliance party but would also have weighed heavily on low-wage families who did pay rates. The borough council was trapped.

Poplar, in common with other London boroughs, paid levies or precepts to the London County Council, the Metropolitan Police, the Asylums Board and the Water Board for services administered throughout London. Poplar's share of about £270,000 was included in the rates paid by householders. Lansbury recorded: 'We met as a Labour Party to try and discover what to do.'[8] At this meeting, which included Labour Guardians as well as Labour councillors, the injustice of the precepts system was raised. It was pointed out that they were not levied according to ability to pay, so that rich and poor boroughs might pay the same amount. Poplar, therefore, was contributing towards the costs of rich boroughs for certain common services but there was no similar pooling to help with poor relief costs which bore most heavily on Poplar. It was agreed that Poplar should refuse to collect and pay that part of the rate accounting for the common services. The objective was two-fold: to press for an 'equalization of the rates' scheme so that rich boroughs contributed to poor ones and to draw national attention to the problem of local government finance.

The intention to break the law predictably provoked fury amongst the Municipal Alliance. It also drew fire from some Labour figures, especially Herbert Morrison, secretary of the London Labour Party, who argued that Labour's reputation would be damaged. Lansbury replied, in the *Herald*, that 'The question is not whether what we are doing is legal or illegal, but whether it is right or wrong'. He added that Conservatives had broken the law by taking up arms in Ulster whereas the illegality he advocated was within a framework of non-violence.[9]

In March 1921, the Poplar council refused its legal obligation to pay precepts. The LCC took legal action and in July the High Court ordered the councillors to pay. The Labour members declined and in September were jailed for contempt of court. Among those sent to Brixton Prison were Lansbury, his son Edgar and two close friends, Charlie Sumner and John Scurr. Five women councillors went to Holloway Prison including Julia Scurr and Minnie Lansbury. George, now in his sixties, soon fell ill, but he refused to go to hospital. He was encouraged by crowds of unemployed people who gathered to sing outside and, within a few minutes, the whole prison was ringing with the strains of the Red Flag. Lansbury raised himself up and was able to address the throng through his cell window.

The government grew uneasy about the imprisonment. Apart from large demonstrations by the unemployed, other London boroughs were threatening to withhold their precepts. More generally, the Labour Party had won a number of by-elections since 1918 and seemed to be increasing its popularity. Sir Alfred Mond, who became minister of health in April 1921, wanted a settlement. After six weeks, the LCC asked the High Court to release the prisoners on the grounds that they were now willing to negotiate a settlement. They were thus freed despite not agreeing to pay.

The prisoners had agreed to attend a London-wide conference to sort out the issue of precepts. More important, Mond carried through the London Authorities (Financial Provision) Act of 1921. While not giving complete equalization of rates, it did mean that out-door relief and some indoor expenses were to be shared through a common fund levied on all the boroughs. Lansbury was well pleased:

> This immediately relieved the rates of Poplar to the extent of 6s 6d in the £ and put 1s in the £ on the rates of Westminster and the City of London. It will thus be seen that although our going to prison was a very inconvenient and not at all pleasant experience for us, it resulted in a very great advantage to the people of Poplar.[10]

The new act also empowered the minister to draw up scales of outdoor relief as a guide to the London area. The Mond scale allowed twenty-five shillings for a man and wife, six shillings for the first child, five shillings for the second and third, and four shillings for others. It was an improvement on the payments of some unions but still inadequate in that no specific provision was made for rent. When the Poplar Guardians applied it, local demonstrations were organized by the Workers' Socialist Federation which regarded Lansbury and the Labour Party as too moderate. On one occasion, its supporters surrounded the Guardians in their office, where Lansbury cheerfully accepted his second 'imprisonment'. Whether due to this pressure or not, the Guardians agreed to more generous rates knowing that Poplar no longer had to foot the full bill. Further, some Guardians were reluctant to apply the means test. As Mrs Julia Scurr explained, working-class Guardians knew how their neighbours were suffering and were 'ashamed to offer the people the amount we offer', and did not want to knock off a few shillings because a means test revealed that a son was delivering groceries for a local shop.[11]

The tactics of the Poplar Guardians, which were followed by some other socialist Boards of Guardians, brought forth a torrent of criticism and abuse from politicians and press. They were accused of wasting public money and encouraging idlers. So strong was the language that Lansbury later stated that one of the reasons for writing *My Life*, published in 1928, was 'to refute the misrepresentation of their activities'.[12] The crescendo of condemnation led the minister of health to appoint H.I. Cooper, an old-style clerk, to the Bolton Guardians, to inquire into the Poplar practices. Cooper interviewed nobody, but his report in 1922 still reproached the Poplar Board for departing from the spirit of the Poor Law and suggested that it could save £100,000 a year by reducing the amount spent on out-relief and on food in the workhouse.

The Guardians responded with a pamphlet, *Guilty and Proud of It*. Father Groser, in recording these events, noted that the pamphlet was prefaced by a biblical text from James 1:27, which read: 'Pure religion and undefiled before God and the Father is this, to visit the fatherless and widows in their affliction.' He added that: 'the thing which first struck me forcibly on coming to Poplar was the essentially religious nature of the revolt which was taking place'.[13] Whether for socialist or Christian reasons, or a combination of both, most Poplar Guardians put their duty to be generous to neighbours above their obligation to keep to the letter of the Poor Law regulations.

The government did not share Groser's sympathies. Mond followed the Cooper inquiry with an order restricting relief to his scale. When ignored, he sent auditors to surcharge Poplar and other Guardians. This particular conflict ended when the Labour Party obtained its first, albeit brief, government in 1924 and John Wheatley, the minister of health, remitted the surcharges. It was replaced by a Conservative government and the next minister, Neville Chamberlain, took powers to suspend uncooperative

Guardians. But the very system of Boards of Guardians was soon to end and the heyday of Poplarism was over.

M.A. Crowther states: 'Poplarism was a political movement associated entirely with the patriarchal figure of George Lansbury, who more than the leaders of his party, represented the conscience of Labour.'[14] Lansbury would have disliked such a personification of Poplarism. In his account of the events, he is at pains to name and praise his fellow Guardians and councillors. Moreover, other Boards of Guardians, particularly at Bedwellty, Chester-le-Street and West Ham, acted in similar fashion. Lansbury's was a leading part, but only a part, of a movement which won enormous publicity and which was debated with great emotion. Poplarism was a highly significant movement.

First, it did not harm Labour's election performances. Some Labour figures feared that Poplarism was a vote loser and J.H. Thomas of the National Union of Railwaymen asserted that it caused Labour's disappointing results in the local elections of 1922. However, in areas where Poplarism was practised, the Labour vote actually held up. In Poplar, Labour won all but one of the Guardians' seats while their councillors won 36 of 42 seats. And, in the 1922 general election, Lansbury won back the Bow and Bromley seat with a resounding majority.

Poplarism also represented a rejection of the Poor Law principles as a means of dealing with poor people. The Poplar Guardians, and some others, attempted to pay recipients of out-relief the maximum rather than the minimum rates possible. They sometimes granted rates in excess of the lowest wages in the borough. At times they refused to apply a stringent means test; and they even gave out-relief to single young people without dependents. Ryan said that 'this version of "Poplarism" rejected the basic assumptions of the deterrent Poor Law; it refused to play the game by the same rules'.[15] Crowther further explains: 'The real conflict between the Ministry and the Poplarists was not administrative: they were making different assumptions about a national minimum standard of living. Lansbury and the Poplar Guardians agreed that the usual rates of outdoor relief were not enough to maintain an unemployed family in health . . .'[16]

Poplarism was thus a challenge to the old Poor Law in that it attempted to relieve poverty according to new and more humane principles. Its practitioners wanted to make payments not at levels so low as to deter others but at levels which met the essential living needs of applicants. Interestingly, this challenge had come from within the Poor Law itself. For most of the previous century, Guardians could be relied upon to uphold the grudging and condemnatory spirit of the 1834 act. The emergence of socialist Guardians changed that and so altered the system from within that the central government was forced to intervene.

Furthermore, Poplarism was associated with the very demise of the Poor Law. As explained in chapter three, Lansbury had a long record of trying to improve the Poor Law from within while simultaneously campaigning for its abolition and replacement by a different system. Poplarism brought the end of the Poor Law ever nearer. The Conservative government found itself in a dilemma. In favour of cutting public expenditure, it was not prepared to let socialist Guardians spend even more on the poor. Yet it did not want to be cast as the upholder of the harsh Victorian Poor Law, particularly as it was often dealing with ex-servicemen and their families who still retained public sympathy. Finally, Neville Chamberlain guided through the Local Government Act of 1929 which handed the responsibility of the Poor Law functions and the roles of the Guardians over to Public Assistance Committees of the local authorities. The Poor Law remained in this form until 1946 and so was no longer the responsibility of parishes.

Moreover, the scope of the Poor Law was diminished as insurance cover was extended to more categories of the population and by the creation of the Unemployment Assistance Board in 1934. This Board's dealings with the unemployed were to involve many conflicts but its formation did indicate that unemployment was recognized as a national rather than a local problem. Lansbury approved, for he had consistently argued that only central government had the resources to deal adequately with unemployment and the powers to establish a system that applied fairly all over the country. Further, he rightly foresaw that these new developments signalled the death throes of the Poor Law. Curiously, they were enacted by a Conservative and then a National government, both of which he bitterly opposed. But Lansbury could take satisfaction that the kind of changes he had advocated in articles, books and numerous speeches were at last coming to fruition. He could even rejoice that the role of Guardian, which he filled for thirty-seven years, was finally abolished. Social policy had moved in the directions outlined in the Minority Report of the

Royal Commission on the Poor Law and in Lansbury's booklet of 1911, aptly titled *Smash the Workhouse*.

Taken up with his statutory duties as Guardian, councillor and sometimes MP, it might be thought that Lansbury would have little time for voluntary bodies. Yet he often expressed admiration for them and supported them whenever possible. As early as 1904, he was a committee member of the London Vacant Land Cultivation Society, started by Joseph Fels, which let out land in West Ham at low rents to working-class people who then successfully grew vegetables and fruit for themselves and for sale. Much later, he strove to raise funds to preserve for Poplar the Elizabethan Sutton House under the auspices of the National Trust. He admired Clara Grant who provided breakfasts for hungry children at her school and who encouraged Margaret MacMillan in the establishment of the first school clinics. In later life, Clara Grant took over as warden of Fern Street Settlement which, she explained, involved 'not the descent of strangers from afar' but 'grew out of the perfectly natural desire of a country-bred teacher to live among her children'.[17] Lansbury was always sympathetic to anything which helped children, and when the Rev. W. Clapham, whose Methodist church was opposite Lansbury's home, could not raise the money for a clinic and nursery school for local children, Lansbury contacted a charitable trust and even the prime minister for help. The clinic and school were eventually opened. Lansbury would back any voluntary effort provided it was not imposed from outside, was not exploited by middle-class officers for their own ends, and was really in the interests of the residents of Poplar.

The bulk of his time, however, was taken up with his official tasks. Priority had to be given to his parliamentary duties but he was also a long-standing member of the Poplar council and served at a time both when, as has just been described, the council was drawn into conflict with central bodies and also when it was establishing municipal socialism. He supported council action which expanded the provision of libraries, parks, street lighting and cleansing, swimming pools and wash-houses. The council took advantage of any government legislation which permitted advances in the provision of school meals, school health services, child welfare clinics and improvements in the quality of education. Lansbury presided at the opening of the Poplar municipal power station, which became an effective and efficient conveyor of electricity to the borough. He readily backed the borough when it compelled some slum landlords to improve their property. He rejoiced at the growth of council housing. He played a leading role in the council's determination to pay decent wages even when threatened with surcharging by the district auditor. After the Law Lords upheld the auditor's decision, the council agreed to reduce wages in return for withdrawal of the surcharge but they continued to pay rates above those of other local authorities.

These advances were being made in other local authorities as well as Poplar. In Great Britain as a whole, the output of council dwellings rose from 63,996 in 1931 to 121,653 in 1939. Advances were dependent upon enabling legislation, and often subsidies, from central government as well as the will of the local government. None the less, the achievements of the Poplar borough council were noteworthy, for it pressed ahead despite having fewer financial resources and greater housing deprivations and levels of unemployment than most other local authorities.

The achievements, remarkable as they were, still left much to be done. Overcrowding was still common, council housing lists were long, poverty was still widespread. But Lansbury perceived real progress, for he remembered the even more extreme suffering of Victorian days.

He compared the improved health of many children in the 1930s with the often stunted growth and disease-racked bodies of many of his schoolmates. He noted that the infant mortality rate in Poplar, although still high compared with more affluent areas, had dropped by 30 per cent under Labour councils. He contrasted the sanitation, space and security of tenure of council housing with the squalor and evictions common to privately rented rooms. He recalled in his younger days 'seeing a bedraggled procession of half-starved women match workers dressed in the most ugly coarse clothes'.[18] By the time he wrote, in 1935, their descendants were represented by trade unions, possessed better clothes and more regular wages. Not least, Lansbury was proud that the borough had improved the quality and quantity of education to the area's children. Moreover, as Noreen Branson explains, some of the policies for which the Labour Poplar Council stood — central grants to supplement local rates, child allowances for families, equal pay for women — have since been fully or partially achieved.[19]

In Lansbury's view, it was not just a matter of what was accomplished in Poplar but who did it. In *My Life*, he expressed the hope that the new generation:

will read the story of Poplarism and recognise that in days when to be destitute and poor was almost a crime, some poor men and women refused to accept that doctrine and together proclaimed the truth that all men are not only born equal, but were also possessed of the inalienable right to share in the products of their labour.[20]

Sharing in the products of their labour also meant deciding how goods, services and resources should be used and distributed. In other words, Lansbury was emphasizing that in Poplar, and elsewhere in the Labour movement it was working-class men and women who were bringing about change. His books are full of references to Poplar people, to the labourers, engineers, postmen, bricklayers and unemployed folk who served as councillors and Guardians. Mention has already been made of Will Crooks who refused the offer of a rent-free house from an admirer with the words, 'My friends among the working people would fear I was deserting their class . . . My enemies would say, "Look at that fellow Crooks; he's making a pile out of us".'[21] Lansbury sorely missed his fellow Guardian when he died in 1921.

At least, as an MP, Crooks' name is still remembered. Others are now only known because Lansbury insisted on giving them credit in his writings. There was Charlie Sumner, a stoker, who, as a councillor, became a first-class administrator with a flair for handling financial matters; John and Julia Scurr, both leading Poplarists; Sam March who, as mayor, led his colleagues into Brixton prison; Charlie Key, a close friend as well as fellow councillor; Will Pearson, an immensely talented docker who was tragically killed in an accident; and many more. Lansbury shared a sense of fraternity with them all and declared:

They helped with slum clearance and housing, supported free compulsory elementary and advanced education for all children. They did this not because they imagined that these things were in themselves Socialism, but because they were things that made the attainment of Socialism more possible.[22]

Lansbury was ever resistant to the doctrine that privileged middle-class experts were the route to social improvement. On the contrary, he perceived that their domination of the top positions in parliament, local government, voluntary bodies and industries was really a means of perpetuating existing social inequalities and class differences. As a result, their actions only marginally improved conditions for working-class people. He therefore insisted that working-class members should fill such positions and he held up their achievements in Poplar as evidence that they possessed both the ability and the will so to do.

These talented councillors, although mainly working class, were from varied backgrounds and included Catholics and Protestants, pacifists and non-pacifists, moderates and militants. Their success depended partly on their unity and it was here that Lansbury made an important contribution to the Poplar Labour Party. His friendships with so many local socialists helped to draw them together. Noreen Branson, in her historical account of these years, explains that he combined laughter with serious determination and so motivated others both to unite and act. At meetings 'he had a unique ability to search out and pursue points of agreement so that matters on which discord could arise receded in importance.'[23] Moreover, his cheerful readiness to chat to anyone in the street and to listen to local deputations did much to maintain support for the Poplar Labour administration.

Lansbury thus took encouragement from the fact that socialism in Poplar provided opportunities for working-class residents to lead the borough and also that it engendered the backing of many ordinary citizens who displayed a sense of responsibility for and solidarity with others going through hard times.

Lansbury remained a councillor for the rest of his life. He was always returned at local elections with a resounding majority, for he had become a part of Poplar itself. The historian Professor Bill Fishman, himself born in the East End as a son of Jewish immigrants, often saw Lansbury in the 1930s and describes him as 'of medium height, piercing blue eyes and always a smile. As he walked along the streets, he spoke to everyone for he was revered in the East End.'[24]

Lansbury's civic offices had thus made him a public figure. It is easy to overlook the fact that he also had a private life. Throughout all these hectic years, he maintained close contact with his children. Edgar reveals that almost every day he would be in touch with one or two, patching up quarrels, advising on baby care of the grandchildren and '. . . being prouder of their minor achievements than of his own part in the affairs of the world'.[25] One of the grandchildren was John Raymond, one of the two sons of Daisy Lansbury and her husband Raymond Postgate. During this period, Daisy often acted as Lansbury's secretary while Raymond was establishing himself as a prominent socialist writer. The grandson John (now Professor Postgate FRS of the University of Sussex) recalls of Lansbury that:

> he was immensely fond of his numerous grandchildren. To us he was a large be-whiskered figure with an East End accent, whose kiss was prickly and uncomfortable, but who usually gave us half a crown at the end of a visit. This to us was true riches: our pocket money was 3d to 6d a week.
>
> GL had a Xmas party for all his grandchildren each year at 39 Bow Road. There'd be games, a Xmas tree, a mighty tea, and Grandma or his daughter Aunt Dolly (Dorothy) would play the piano and we'd sing community songs. The rooms and the dark, velvety or leathery furniture were full of children, aunts and uncles. The grandchildren greatly enjoyed it all.[26]

Along with the family joys came some pain. Edgar's wife, Minnie, was one of the councillors who went to prison. She died a few months later and George remained convinced that the experience contributed to the early death of this talented woman. Edgar, also a councillor, succeeded his father as chair of the Poplar Guardians but soon after was named as the co-respondent in a divorce case involving a well-known actress, Moyna MacGill. They married in September 1924 and by November they were mayor and mayoress of Poplar. But the bitter-sweet events were not over. Edgar had taken on the wood mill business in conjunction with brother William, who was happy to allow him the time for Guardian and council business. In 1925, the business failed and the brothers were declared bankrupt. George had little money and could not give financial help. However, Edgar later recorded that in this, as in the divorce case, he loyally supported his son, offering no words of reproach and many of encouragement. Then, in 1928, Lansbury's brother James was killed by a train at Forest Gate station — whether by accident or suicide was never clearly established. Also about this time, the exact date is uncertain, his youngest brother,

Harry, died when a minor foot injury became infected. Sometimes George felt tired and worn and considered that his life was almost over. Yet, by this time, he was back in the Commons and about to become even more prominent in national politics.

References

[1] A.J.P. Taylor, *English History 1914–1945*, Penguin Books, reprinted 1987, p. 275, note 3.

[2] P. Romero, *E. Sylvia Pankhurst*, Yale University Press, 1987, p. 93.

[3] St J. Groser, *Politics and Persons*, SCM Press, 1949, p. 69.

[4] C. Grant, *From Me to We*, Fern Street Settlement, 1940, chapter 3.

[5] Cited in N. Middleton, *When Family Failed*, Gollancz, 1971, p. 151.

[6] W. Hannington, *Black Coffins and the Unemployed*, Fact Books, 1939.

[7] R. Postgate, *The Life of George Lansbury*, Longmans, Green & Co., 1951, p. 217.

[8] G. Lansbury, *My Life*, Constable, 1928, p. 155.

[9] Cited by N. Branson, *Poplarism 1919–1925*, Lawrence Wishart, 1979, p. 57.

[10] Lansbury, *My Life*, p. 161.

[11] Cited in P. Ryan, 'Poplarism 1894–1930' in P. Thane (ed.), *The Origins of British Social Policy*, Croom Helm, 1978, p. 79.

[12] Lansbury, *My Life*, p. 1.

[13] St J. Groser, *Politics and Persons*, p. 22.

[14] M.A. Crowther, *The Workhouse System 1834–1929*, Batsford Academic, 1981, p. 105.

[15] P. Ryan, 'Poplarism', p. 77.

[16] M.A. Crowther, *The Workhouse System*, p. 106.

[17] C. Grant, *From Me to We*, p. 41.

[18] G. Lansbury, *Looking Backwards and Forwards*, Blackie and Son Ltd., 1935, p. 56.

[19] N. Branson, *op. cit.*, pp. 227–28.

[20] Lansbury, *My Life*, p. 287.

[21] Cited in G. Haw, *From Workhouse to Westminster. The Life Story of Will Crooks MP*, Cassell & Co. Ltd., 1907, pp. 82–83.

22   Lansbury, *Looking Backwards*, p. 238.

23   N. Branson, *Poplarism 1919–1925*, p. 167.

24   Professor W. Fishman, recorded interview with the author.

25   E. Lansbury, *George Lansbury, My Father*, Sampson Low, Marston & Co., 1934, p. 152.

26   Professor J. Postgate, letter to the author.

7

IN THE CABINET

Following the collapse of the post-war coalition government, the 1922 general election was fought on party lines. It resulted in a Conservative government headed by Bonar Law, who was soon replaced by Stanley Baldwin.

The election saw the Labour Party representation rise to 142 seats. A number of the new MPs were from middle-class backgrounds, including Clement Attlee, so the parliamentary party was no longer dominated by working-class, trade union nominees. There was also a strengthening of the 'Red Clydesiders', who were working class, Scottish, and eager for a socialist revolution. When parliament opened, MacDonald led for Labour. He was followed, wrote John McNair in his biography of James Maxton, 'by that great Christian Socialist, George Lansbury, and even the thirty-year-old pages of *Hansard* vibrate with the warmth of his appeal on behalf of the unemployed'.[1] Then the Red Clydesiders, Maxton, John Wheatley, Emanuel Shinwell and David Kirkwood, rose to list the sufferings of their constituents.

Back in the Commons after ten years, Lansbury was, as Austen Morgan states, 'the major left wing figure . . . he was now the hero of municipal resistance'.[2] He again felt irritated by the formality and conventions of the Commons. He resented the readiness of some of his socialist colleagues to attend and dress up for the parties and gatherings arranged by the establishment. He wrote:

> I cannot think the Labour Party fulfills its mission by proving how adaptable we are and how nicely we can dress and behave when we enter official, royal and upper circles. It seems to me we would do better to try to order our lives on the same lines as before we became members of Parliament.[3]

Yet now Lansbury did not let these feelings spoil his performances in the Commons. A member of the Labour Party's Executive Committee, he soon found himself on the party's front bench where he proved an effective as well as a passionate speaker.

Faced with economic difficulties, Baldwin went to the country at the end of 1923 advocating protectionism rather than free trade as the answer to the crisis. The outcome gave the Conservatives 258, Labour 191 and Liberals 159 seats. No party had an overall majority and, in January 1924, the king asked MacDonald to form a minority government.

With himself taking the foreign office, MacDonald appointed Snowden as chancellor of the exchequer, Henderson as home secretary, Wheatley as health minister, and Webb as president of the Board of Trade. In all, as A.J.P. Taylor observes, 'It marked a social revolution . . . working men in a majority, the great public schools and the old universities eclipsed for the first time.'[4] Yet, as Sydney Webb recorded:

> The one glaring omission, so the Labour Party thought, was George Lansbury, who had certainly established a position in the party entitling him to Cabinet rank . . . I felt his exclusion to be a mistake, and so did Henderson, who also criticised it to MacDonald; and so it proved.[5]

Why did MacDonald keep Lansbury out? King George had been offended by a public remark of Lansbury's which referred to the fate of Charles I when he stood in the way of the public will. MacDonald also wanted to distance his cabinet from extremists and Pelling pointed out of Lansbury that 'several members of his family were communists, and he himself had only lately been in prison'.[6] The point is an exaggeration for only Violet and Edgar Lansbury were fully identified with the Communist Party while Lansbury's imprisonment, along with that of the other Poplar councillors, had won him the backing rather than the condemnation of many working-class people. But MacDonald was fearful that sneers about extremists and communists would harm the Labour Party's electoral prospects so Lansbury, along with most other left wingers, was kept out of the government.

The appointment of the first Labour government had been greeted with initial enthusiasm by Labour supporters. As he left Glasgow for the Commons, David Kirkwood stated, 'Bishops, financiers, lawyers, and all the polite spongers upon the working classes know that this is the beginning of the end.'[7] The more realistic MacDonald, however, knew that a minority government could only go as far as the opposition parties would allow it. His tactic was to proceed cautiously, to give ministerial experience to Labour MPs, and to convince the country that a socialist administration could be moderate and responsible. It was certainly moderate, and few innovations occurred. No new policies were introduced to deal with unemployment and Sydney Webb frankly admitted, 'I certainly failed to do any lasting good in this field.'[8] The most successful minister turned out to be the one Red Clydesider in the cabinet, John Wheatley. He advanced council house building by increasing the subsidy for houses to nine pounds a year for forty years and by insisting that they be built for rent. Abroad, MacDonald proved an able negotiator. He mediated between France and Germany over the question of reparations, supported the League of Nations, and recognized the Soviet government.

Lansbury was deeply disappointed at the government's lack of progress, although he was enthusiastic about Wheatley's performance. He disagreed with MacDonald's tactic and argued that Labour should have brought forward genuine socialist proposals, such as the nationalization of the mines. When defeated in the Commons, the party should have appealed to the country. These views were expressed in the *Herald* and served to fuel MacDonald's obsession that extremists and communists were taking over the Labour Party.

Oddly enough, it was the cabinet's apparent pro-communist bias which brought about its downfall. In recognizing the Soviet government, MacDonald had promised a commercial treaty and a loan. Lloyd George seized the opportunity to declare how shocking it was to support the Bolsheviks. Then, J.R. Campbell, the editor of a communist weekly, was charged with publishing a 'Don't shoot' appeal to soldiers brought in to deal with strikers. Such appeals were often published and Labour backbenchers persuaded the attorney-general to drop the charges against Campbell — himself a wounded war veteran. The Conservatives condemned the withdrawal as political interference to save a communist. With Liberal support, they defeated the government and MacDonald resigned. The first Labour government had lasted less than a year.

During the next election, as the historian Thomson states,

'Conservative propaganda had worked hard to equate the Labour Party with communism.'[9] Lansbury's visits to Russia and his praises of the achievements there were cited as evidence. Four days before the poll, the *Daily Mail* published a letter, supposedly from Zinoviev, president of the Communist International, giving instructions to the British Communist Party to undertake various seditious activities. The letter, almost certainly a fake, did not reduce the overall Labour vote but it did seem to bring out more Consevative voters. The outcome was Conservatives 419 seats, Labour 151, and Liberals, the real losers, down to 40. As for Lansbury, he held Bow and Bromley comfortably albeit with a reduced majority.

The Conservatives' overall majority did at least ensure a government which lasted five years. Baldwin as prime minister and Churchill as chancellor of the exchequer were its leading figures, although Seaman concluded that 'not only was it a Government without a policy: it was a government without new talent'.[10] But in terms of legislation, the most influential figure turned out to be the minister of health, Neville Chamberlain, who piloted twenty-one acts through the Commons. Lansbury, in opposition, was magnanimous enough to welcome some of Chamberlain's reforms. In particular, he supported provisions within the Local Government Act of 1929 which abolished the Board of Guardians system and transferred the functions of the Poor Law to public assistance committees of local authorities. However, he pointed out that the Poor Law had been improved, not abolished, and that poverty still marred the lives of many whose only refuge was still the hated Poor Law. Similarly, Lansbury was thankful when the government jettisoned the sacred cow of the insurance principle and made unemployment benefit a statutory right for a longer period than that for which contributions had been paid. Yet he also criticized the low levels of the benefits and attacked the condition imposed by legislation that recipients had to be 'genuinely seeking work'. It was not that Lansbury was against men seeking work but rather that he knew that the rigid application of such a test would discriminate against people who had no hope of finding a job.

Lansbury never confined himself to comment on home affairs. When the government informed Soviet Russia that it would not be proceeding with the recognition initiated by the Labour administration, he condemned their action as foolish both politically and economically. Politically because it could endanger the peace between the two countries and economically because it hampered trade relations which could have benefited both nations. He continued to foster the cause of self-rule for British colonies, particularly in India, and he helped form the Labour Commonwealth Group which sought to establish a more equal relationship between Britain and her empire. Interestingly, Lansbury also advocated that 'Scotland, Wales and England should each have their own Parliament with a joint committee for matters concerning them all'.[11]

It was not events abroad but those at home which created the biggest challenge for the Conservative government. It was alarmed by unemployment and the fall in exports. Ministers reasoned that if employers' costs were cut then the prices of goods could be reduced so enabling them to compete abroad and increase exports. If exports and trade flourished then unemployment would drop. Employers' main costs were wages, so the government advocated wage cuts — or, at least, no wage increases. A.J.P. Taylor explains that the analysis was faulty for markets abroad were being lost for other reasons — such as the growth of industries in countries to which Britain had previously exported goods — and that wages in the export industries were already low so that 'further reduction, by weakening the home market, would have caused more unemployment than it cured'.[12] Among the few commentators who perceived this point at the time were the economist John Maynard Keynes, the trade unionist Ernie Bevin, and Lansbury. The government never accepted this view and, in 1925, Baldwin announced that all workers would have to take cuts in income. Inevitably, the focus turned on Britain's largest industry, the coal mines, which employed over a million workers.

The miners refused to accept the lower wages and longer hours stipulated by the coal owners and were then locked out. In May 1926, the General Council of the TUC called a national strike, known as the General Strike, in their support. Under the drive of Ernie Bevin of the Transport and General Workers Union, over two million workers responded. A.J.P. Taylor draws attention to the 'nobility' of these strikers who 'asked nothing for themselves. They did not seek to challenge the government, still less to overthrow the constitution. They merely wanted the miners to have a living wage.'[13] The government replied by drafting in volunteers and the armed forces to maintain supplies. The TUC soon gave way and accepted the need for wage cuts in return for a better organization of the mining industry (which was never made). The miners held out for a further six months until starvation drove them back to lower wages and longer hours. The government followed their victory with legislation which outlawed any strikes designed to 'coerce' the government.

Through all this, Lansbury gave his full support to the strikers. He defended them in the Commons, he attacked the Conservatives for tolerating the hunger of miners' children, and he raised funds for the miners' cause. Yet he acknowledged that the General Strike had been a failure, a failure which further confirmed that industrial action would not bring about profound political change. He thus worked even harder to win support for a democratically elected Labour government as the means to change.

A democratically elected Labour government would have Mac-Donald at its head. MacDonald was still the undisputed leader, respected for his tactical skills in holding his parliamentary colleagues together, admired for his great orations at Labour Party conferences, and almost revered for his distinction in being the first-ever Labour premier. Yet MacDonald had never given his whole-hearted support to the strikers, for not only was he keen to disassociate his party with a militancy which might alienate moderate voters; he also appeared to accept the case for lower wages. Indeed, throughout this period, Baldwin and MacDonald drew closer together as it emerged that they held similar views on a number of issues. By contrast, MacDonald was anxious to distance himself from some sections of his own party. He abhorred Lansbury's uncompromising backing for strikers and considered that his views, often expressed in the *Herald*, tainted the Labour Party with the stigma of the communists who also fervently supported the General Strike. Lansbury, for his part, thought that MacDonald was diluting socialism and failing to present the Labour Party to the public as an option quite distinct from the other parties.

The differences were made clear in Lansbury's *My Life*, published in 1928. Baldwin, Chamberlain, even MacDonald might be satisfied with improvements in the standards of working-class life. Certainly, under the Conservative administration improvements had been made to old-age pensions and much of the population was enjoying a higher standard of living. It was often claimed that destitution was disappearing, that overcrowding was falling and that the expansion of insurance schemes was providing an alternative to the Poor Law for more people. Lansbury welcomed all these advances and, indeed, he promoted some of them. But he did not consider them sufficient. He perceived that, although the living conditions of poor people might be improving slowly, the social and material gap between them and the rest of the population was not diminishing, for standards were rising for all of society. In short, Lansbury wanted not slight improvements but greater equality. Thus his book is a testimony to his understanding of socialism. He called for 'absolute equality of remuneration to all, so as to ensure an equal standard of life as a right to all who serve the nation, no matter in what position they serve'.[14] He knew that all people could not be identical, for he understood that all individuals possess different abilities and needs. He perceived that they must do different tasks, with some teaching children, some cleaning sewers and so on. But he added that all should have the same status and all live in the same healthy environments. Lansbury wanted a Labour Party that openly proclaimed these objectives, not one that appeared just a bit more sympathetic to the working class than the Conservatives.

Lansbury wanted public ownership of industry and the replacement of capitalism by socialism not as ends in themselves but as means of promoting equality, co-operation and fraternity. To MacDonald, much of this seemed an extremism which would frighten the British voter. Whether this was so or not, it did not diminish Lansbury's standing within the Labour Party for he was elected its chairman for 1927–28.

Following its victory in the General Strike, the Conservative Party had high hopes of further success in the general election of 1929. With the support of both private firms and many wealthy individuals, it had far more money for political organization than the other parties. In terms of propaganda, it benefited from the support of seven of the ten daily newspapers and all but one of the Sunday newspapers. Yet its anti-trade union legislation ensured that Labour supporters remained loyally behind their party while its harsh policies towards the unemployed, not all of whom were working class, alienated some traditional Conservative voters. Moreover, this election was the first one based on universal suffrage for women as well as men. The result, a magnificent one for Labour, was Labour 288 seats, Conservatives 260, and Liberals 59. In Bow and Bromley, the Municipal Alliance had formed a fund to back the Conservative candidate against Lansbury whom they blamed for the increase in local rates. Their fund and abuse was of no avail. Lansbury's popularity in the East End now made his seat unassailable and he was returned again.

Once more MacDonald was prepared to lead a minority government. Arthur Henderson took the foreign office, Snowden the treasury, Clynes the home office and Thomas became Lord Privy Seal. Margaret Bondfield, as minister of labour, had the distinction of being the first woman member of a British cabinet. In junior posts, the future generation of Labour leaders began to make their mark with the likes of Herbert Morrison, Hugh Dalton, Emanuel Shinwell and later Clem Attlee and Stafford Cripps. As before, MacDonald was prepared to accept one left winger in the cabinet and this time he could not ignore the claims of George Lansbury, who became first commissioner of works.

Lansbury's supporters sent him many congratulations on his appointment. His old friend, Commissioner David Lamb of the Salvation Army, wrote in excited fashion:

> I regard this day as perhaps the greatest in our lifetime. In August 1914 our civilisation went to pieces and you and your colleagues have now the opportunities of doing something substantial not only to restore but to advance 'the kingdom', to create 'a new heaven and a new earth'.

A 'new heaven and a new earth', however, were not on the political agenda of the dominant cabinet figures of MacDonald, Snowden, Thomas and Clynes. MacDonald was the undisputed leader. As Michael Foot puts it, 'He stood head and shoulders above all rivals, the clear master of his Party.'[15] And MacDonald was insistent that the strategy again had to be that of staying in power as long as possible in order to persuade the electorate that they were fit to be returned with an overall majority. Such an approach entailed pursuing only those measures which would win the support of the Liberal minority.

Initially small increases were made in some unemployment insurance benefits while a Housing Act provided subsidies for local authorities to proceed with slum clearance schemes. Abroad, Henderson resumed diplomatic relations with Russia and paved the way for a European conference on disarmament. Despite setbacks, the government also encouraged negotiations towards Indian independence. But these steps in no way fulfilled the election manifesto which had promised the nationalization of certain industries and an all-out attack on unemployment. It certainly did not satisfy James Maxton, a brilliant orator from Glasgow, who had considerable support from other Red Clydesiders and the remnant of the Independent Labour Party which still sponsored some MPs. They wanted the government to increase unemployment pay substantially and to nationalize the declining cotton industry and, if defeated, to go to the country in another general election. Instead they found Margaret Bondfield executing unemployment policies akin to those of the Conservatives – a point made in the Commons by a Labour newcomer, Aneurin Bevan, who also drew her attention to the suffering of his constituents in Ebbw Vale. Maxton, as Gordon Brown explains in his biography, grew more and more exasperated and was soon asking, 'Has any human being benefited by the fact there has been a Labour Government in office?'[16]

Lansbury felt sympathy for Maxton with whom he had often shared platforms. Indeed, some Labour members felt that MacDonald had shunted Lansbury into the minor cabinet post of first commissioner for works to prevent him teaming up with Maxton to form a formidable duo of backbench critics. But Lansbury had accepted the job and was determined to make the most of it. Every day he caught the bus or underground from Bow to Whitehall, where he began to galvanize what had been a stuffy government department. To the civil servants, the brief of the Office of Works was to conserve and maintain old buildings and royal parks. To Lansbury, it presented the opportunity to promote play and recreation. As a child and then as a father, Lansbury had enjoyed Victoria Park where children from overcrowded homes could play in spacious grounds. He later wrote, 'The theory that children of the poor do not know how to play is not true.'[17] He added that the trouble was that they lacked places where they could play. He thus cast his eye over the London parks and decided that for too long they had been monopolized by the middle- and upper-classes. As his plans for opening them up to poor people became clear, the civil servants, still steeped in Victorian traditions, reacted with horror. Postgate tells that he would meet their objections in this way:

Well, brother, you've given a very fine explanation of what *can't* be done. Now I want you just to sit down and work out what *can* be done.[18]

Lansbury soon grasped the contents of wordy files, listened patiently to deputations, took into account the views of his staff, and made speedy decisions. Thus his affability and ability won over the civil servants and the permanent secretary, Sir Lionel Earle, became a close friend. Interestingly, Lansbury also related well with King George V with whom he had to discuss the royal parks. Despite one George's fear of socialism and the other George's dislike of inherited power, they chatted together as two elderly men concerned about their country, about the well-being of children, and about each other's health.

Under Lansbury's direction, railings were pulled down, shelters for parents put up, paddling and swimming pools for children constructed, play and recreational equipment installed in the parks over which he had jurisdiction. Mixed bathing was allowed in the Serpentine and Hyde Park was revamped as 'Lansbury's Lido'. His aim was to make the parks attractive to and open to families of all kinds — and he succeeded.

In his brief tenure, most of his work concentrated on London. But Lansbury also had a vision of making all the public parks, pastures and amenities of Britain accessible to all the people. He wanted castles to become children's centres, stately homes to be open to all to enjoy, and camping sites all over the country in order to facilitate cheap holidays for hikers and bikers. He initiated a committee to investigate the setting up of a commission to take charge of all the national parks — an objective which came to fruition after he left office. The energy and enthusiasm of a man now in his seventies was astonishing. And it was an enthusiasm which was not just restricted to his time in office. Later, in 1932, he was elected a vice-president of the National Trust and its minutes reveal that he served on its council, where he maintained his determination that the nation's heritage of history and beauty should be within reach of working-class people.

Lansbury's popularizing of the parks drew some criticisms. The *Morning Post* considered he was attracting hooligans to them. *The Times* sneered that he was turning Hyde Park into Coney Island. When the provision of a children's boating lake and swings at Regent's Park began to draw in children from Camden Town and St Pancras, the wealthy residents adjacent to the park sent a deputation to protest. Lansbury overruled it. He did the same to the objections of the London Free Church Federation to his decision to allow the restaurant at Hampton Court to sell alcohol with meals. Although a total abstainer himself, Lansbury reasoned that he should not force his abstinence upon others.

Generally, however, Lansbury's reforms won support and the press gave much publicity to his efforts. Thus *Time & Tide*, in a long editorial on 29 September 1929, stated that he was probably

> the busiest member of the Government. His first hints of schemes for changes in the London parks were not taken seriously. His mention of an all-British Lido was, even in the heat wave, a journalistic joke. But, if Mr Lansbury is an incorrigible dreamer, there are signs that he is one whose pertinacity makes dreams come true . . . Mr Lansbury is one of those Ministers whose names should have a permanent place in history, and, especially in books of history for children. He will be remembered, it may be, as the First Commissioner for Good Works.

The title 'First Commissioner for Good Works' stuck. His example inspired some local authorities to expand and improve their parks and often Lansbury would be asked to open them. Never had he enjoyed such a good press. His photo, ever smiling, appeared regularly as he kicked-off at football matches, opened boxing gyms, tried out new swings and waved children off on their holidays. Michael Foot, in an interview with the writer, stated that Lansbury was 'just about the only minister who was really successful and who made a mark with the public.'

This mark was recognized by the BBC, who invited him to talk about his work in one of the first transatlantic broadcasts in 1931. In it, Lansbury described his love for parks and gardens and proclaimed his belief that the beauty and space of the natural environment should be available to all. The visual enjoyment of trees and flowers and the physical enjoyment of swimming pools and playing fields, he continued, should help us

> to arrange our lives in such a manner as will ensure that all our faculties of mind and body may be used for the glory of the human race, which in turn means the glory of God.

On the wireless, as in the public hall, Lansbury's strong working-class voice enunciated simple yet profound sentiments which struck a chord in many hearts. Letters poured in, particularly from the

United States and Canada, expressing appreciation. One from Ontario must have given him great pleasure for it said:

> Well, comrade, let me explain that I am one of your converts to the socialist ranks in those tough early days . . . we have lived in London and well we know the boon of those open spaces to the poor.

His post as first commissioner gave Lansbury the opportunity to exercise responsibility and to make decisions which were acted upon. He revealed the capacity to promote policies rather than just to react to events. He won over both the civil servants and the public. It was his and the country's loss that this brief tenure was to be his only experience in ministerial office.

Lansbury's success at the Office of Works gave him some compensation for the difficulties and frustrations he endured within the cabinet. He wanted the government to undertake imaginative socialistic legislation that would win over the public. It was at a public meeting that he spoke in favour of turning the coal mines into a public corporation. MacDonald immediately reminded him that ministers should not pronounce upon policies which had not full approval of the cabinet. Lansbury had to apologize.

Just as frustrating was his experience on a small committee appointed by MacDonald to draw up plans to tackle unemployment. Chaired by J.H. Thomas, it also contained two junior ministers, Tom Johnston and a convert from the Conservatives, the wealthy Sir Oswald Mosley. Margaret Bondfield, in her autobiography, points out how odd and foolish was her exclusion, as the minister of labour, from the committee. She adds, and she was not a vindictive person, that Thomas, although once an able trade union official, 'was not the type of man needed for such a tremendous task'.[19] Indeed, at times Thomas did not seem to take the matter seriously for he believed the economic position would improve. Consequently, the government's action, mainly small public works schemes, made little impact on overall unemployment.

Far from improving, a great economic depression was surfacing in October 1929. An immediate cause lay with British reliance upon American loans and markets. When the United States had its own slump, it cut down on British business, goods and shipping. As British exports decreased so unemployment increased, rising to over two million. The Labour cabinet had few ideas. One man did come up with an economic blueprint, Sir Oswald Mosley. In his account, Mosley explained that his plan contained two parts. In the short term, he wanted large-scale works schemes for 300,000 jobs, an emergency pension scheme for older workers whose retirement would vacate another 280,000 jobs, and raising the school leaving age. All of this to be financed by loans. In the long term, he wanted more public control of industry, planned foreign trade, and the deliberate use of credit to promote economic growth. He even spoke of 'an European economy' in words which foreshadowed the idea of a European Common Market.[20] Mosley's plans, A.J.P. Taylor comments, 'were an astonishing achievement, evidence of a superlative talent which was later to be wasted'.[21] What was Lansbury's reaction to the plan? Mosley recorded that Lansbury was initially suspicious of him, a rich man who joined the socialists, but that once he perceived the value of the scheme he 'fought like a tiger for it'.[22] Lansbury took the Mosley plan to the cabinet, apparently with Thomas' approval, where Snowden dismissed it out of hand. As Seaman observes, it was curious that a Labour chancellor 'had the mentality of a Poor Law Commissioner of the late 1830s'.[23] More orthodox than even Conservative chancellors, he could think only in terms of cutting public expenditure. The proposal to reduce unemployment by taking on loans was anathema to him. Eventually, the cabinet rejected Mosley's proposals and he resigned from the unemployment committee. He then took them to the parliamentary Labour Party and the Labour Party conference where the majority, much influenced by MacDonald's powers of persuasion, remained loyal to the leadership. In 1931, Mosley lost patience and went to form the New Party which turned into a fascist organization.

Lansbury felt trapped in a quandary. He considered resigning but recalled his mistake of 1912 and determined to fight on within the cabinet. But that meant accepting the decisions of MacDonald who, in 1930, assigned him the task of defending the cabinet's policy on unemployment to the Labour Party conference. In his speech, Lansbury asked for the Mosley plan to be circulated and discussed, he pointed to the government's public works schemes, and he explained that a minority government was unable to take full socialist measures to deal with unemployment. Lansbury was embarrassed at the cabinet's lack of action and his speech lacked his usual conviction. Some colleagues reproached him and he was even howled down at a public meeting in Poplar. In many ways the criticisms were unjust, for within the cabinet Lansbury continued to argue for increased public expenditure to reduce unemployment and strongly opposed suggestions that unemployment benefits be cut. Loyalty to the cabinet prevented him from revealing to the public the battle he was waging within the government. MacDonald probably gained some satisfaction from making Lansbury — the left wing critic who had often attacked his policies in the columns of the *Herald* — take on the task of defending a cabinet which had overruled him.

A desperate Lansbury wrote a letter to the *News Chronicle*. It was published on 14 January 1931 and called on the churches to support a complete reorganization of industry so that all workers and their dependents might enjoy decent lives. It was his way of showing that he still wanted socialist measures to combat unemployment. The following month he wrote to Lloyd George — surely without MacDonald's knowledge — urging him to join the Labour Party and to bring in his proposals for large-scale programmes to create jobs. Lloyd George's reply of 16 February is in the Lansbury Collection. He wrote that 'coming over' would not help and added that unless the cabinet adopted some of Lansbury's 'faith and courage' then there would be 'an overwhelming catastrophe'.

That catastrophe seemed ever nearer. As other countries imposed tariffs on imported goods so Britain lost more of its overseas markets. Particularly badly hit were the already declining industries of cotton goods and steel. Prices fell at home and unemployment reached 2,750,000 by July 1931. Snowden had appointed an economy committee under Sir George May. Dominated by industrialists, its report of July 1931 estimated an enormous budget deficit and recommended savings on expenditure by cutting all salaries of persons employed by the state and a 20 per cent reduction in unemployment benefit. Far from helping, the report stimulated fears of a financial collapse and foreign investors became less inclined to put money into Britain.

The cabinet was now split in two. MacDonald, Snowden and Thomas led one faction which accepted the May proposals and believed that public expenditure had to be cut in order to achieve a balanced budget which would restore foreign confidence and investment in Britain. Lansbury won Henderson over and they led the other faction. In an article written later in the *Herald* of 23 October 1931, Lansbury gave some details of the cabinet battle. His side argued that the importance of a balanced budget was overstated, that Britain was not bankrupt, and that any economies could be made by taxing capital gains and high salaries, the proceeds of which should then be invested in industry. In particular, they wanted to shield the unemployed from further suffering. Lansbury found Snowden quite inflexible and considered that he was in the hands of civil servants themselves still gripped by Victorian economics. In the article, he wrote of Snowden, 'Once he has been told what to say and do by the Treasury officials he never budges.'

Outside of the cabinet, the TUC was insisting that any financial sacrifices should apply to unearned incomes and private salaries as well as public wages. Conservatives and some Liberals, however, supported the May recommendations and implied that some of the workless were there by choice, so cuts in unemployment benefit would drive them back to jobs. They repeated the old argument that cuts in wages would reduce employers' costs and so make them more competitive with foreign firms. MacDonald and Snowden now shared these views and so found themselves at one not with the TUC and many Labour supporters but with their political opponents.

The final crunch came when New York bankers insisted on public cuts before they would make further loans available. Snowden considered that American backing was essential to ensure confidence in the economy and to check drains on the gold reserves. Later, in the *Herald* article of October, Lansbury scornfully describes the British cabinet awaiting a telephone call from the American bankers as symbolic of the fact that its leaders were no longer in control. The cabinet divisions now came to a head with eleven going along with MacDonald and Snowden and nine ready to resign rather than accept the cuts. MacDonald therefore had little choice but to end the existing administration and it was assumed that he would make way for a Conservative-Liberal coalition.

But MacDonald did not resign the premiership. After seeing the king, he agreed to head a National Government to meet the economic crisis. Apparently the idea originated with Herbert Samuel, who was leading the Liberals during Lloyd George's illness. The new cabinet consisted of four Labour members, MacDonald, Snowden, Thomas and Sankey, four Conservatives including Baldwin, and two Liberals including Samuel.

MacDonald probably believed that savage cuts and orthodox economics were the only solution. However, he did not wish to allow the Conservatives and Liberals to carry through the policies. His biographer, Austen Morgan, reckons that MacDonald 'believed he was indispensable as Prime Minister. He saw himself as the saviour of the nation at that critical time.'[24] Unkinder critics point to MacDonald's increasing desire to be numbered with high society: a desire which had replaced his commitment to socialism. But whatever the explanation, one fact is certain: MacDonald had not consulted with the majority of his Labour colleagues, who were astonished by his decision.

Thus, whereas the Conservatives and Liberals entered the coalition as parties, MacDonald and his handful of followers entered as individuals. MacDonald's 'betrayal', as it became known in Labour circles, was not just about his readiness to accept the recommendations of the May Committee and the dictates of the banks. After all, some Labour MPs shared his position. It was rather that he had ended a Labour government and taken over the leadership of what was predominantly a Conservative National Government, without the leave of most of the Labour MPs who had supported him, the party members who had worked for him, and the Labour public who had voted for him.

The Labour administration of 1929–31 was finished. Historians have little praise for its achievements. Hugh Dalton, a junior member of the government, agreed that its 'record abroad is a moderate success story . . . Its record at home is a hard-luck story with failure almost unredeemed by courage or skill.'[25]

The newspapers of the time made similar judgments. But a number made one exception. The *Glasgow Evening Citizen* declared:

> It is agreed by everyone that at the Office of Works Mr
> Lansbury has displayed more imagination than any previous
> First Commissioner and future generations will have him to
> thank for improving many of the public amenities in the parks
> under his control.

Even the *Evening Times*, so often a critic of Lansbury's socialism and which mocked him as 'Old Muddlehead' over his pacifism, admitted that he 'was the one Minister to retire with laurels'. But such praise must have meant little to Lansbury. He had spent much of his life striving for a Labour government which would pass socialist legislation. Yet the one cabinet to which he had belonged had done little except copy Conservative economics.

He had seen this minority government as a launching pad to a large Labour majority at the next election. Instead, he witnessed his beloved Labour Party torn in two.

The disappointment might have finished many men of Lansbury's age and persuaded them to retire and enjoy a few years of leisure. Certainly, George could have occupied himself fully with his numerous children, grandchildren, nieces and nephews. It is worth noting that, even during his busy life as MP and cabinet minister, he showed kindness to all of his extended family. His brother Harry had left a widow in poor health with two daughters and no income. The two girls went out to work with the younger, Jessie, having to go into the sweated hat industry, earning ninepence for every completed hat. Each Christmas Day, without fail, George sent the widow a card and a pound note. In anticipation of it, the family would buy a little beef as their Christmas dinner. When the other daughter, Grace, got married, it was George who gave her away.[26] Yet, for all his family commitments, George would not stop his socialist activities. He was determined to continue the fight with Labour.

The fact that George Lansbury was able to carry on depended very much on the backing he received from factors outside of political circles. His family was very important. George gave much time and effort to the family but he also received tremendous support from its members. Especially did this apply to his dear Bessie. In 1930, they celebrated their fiftieth wedding anniversary. The Lansbury Collection contains hundreds of communications of congratulations. They came from the king, from his old friend Wait Sewell, from numerous churches, mission halls, trade unions and sports clubs. And, ironically, from Ramsay MacDonald. Bessie's love and loyalty was such as to sustain him even through the dark days of desertion by lifelong colleagues.

His Christianity was undoubtedly a source of strength. In his biography, published in 1928, he devoted much space to his beliefs. He explained that he had found 'that the fulfillment of life was service of God through service of man' and he urged readers to 'understand that social activities connected with wages, housing, unemployment, status, and conditions of life of the workers very intimately concern the Kingdom of Heaven on earth'.[27] In January 1930, while still a cabinet minister, he wrote in the *Baptist Times*:

Our Lord's message rings in our ears, simple, all pervading

and true, 'Do unto others as ye would they should do unto
you' . . . Love one another, follow after Christ, live in peace
and harmony, each one helping the other, asking no favour
and no privilege above what we will concede and give to our
neighbour . . .

In other words, Lansbury was convinced that, in his political life,
he was following the way of his God and that encouraged him
through all the hard work and through all the set-backs and
sorrows.

Finally, there was the backing and warmth of the ordinary folk
who lived around him in Bow. In the midst of the traumatic
events of 1931, he wrote in the *Daily Sketch* of 18 July that
year:

In a way, I owe most to the fact that I have lived for 64 years in
the East End and so have learnt to know the infinite courage and
kindness of the poor.

As he waited for the bus, walked the streets, opened his door to
the knocks, Lansbury felt closer than ever to his people. He
witnessed the way they helped each other. He appreciated the
encouragements they gave to him, the handshakes, the slaps on
the back, the cheery greetings. Sometimes he looked out of his
window and saw unemployed men hanging around. He could not
stop now. He had to pick up the pieces of the Labour Party
again.

References

1   J. McNair, *James Maxton*, Allen and Unwin, 1955, p. 107.

2   A. Morgan, *J. Ramsey MacDonald*, Manchester University Press, 1987, p. 108.

3   G. Lansbury, *My Life*, Constable, 1928, p. 268.

4   A.J.P. Taylor, *English History 1940–1945*, Penguin Books, reprinted 1987, p. 270.

5   S. Webb, 'The First Labour Government', *Political Quarterly*, vol. xxxii, 1961,
    pp. 13–14.

6   H. Pelling, 'Governing Without Power', *Political Quarterly*, vol. xxxii, 1961, p. 48.

7 Cited in D. Thomson, *England in the Twentieth Century*, Jonathan Cape, 1964, p. 79.

8 Webb, 'The First Labour Government', p. 21.

9 Thomson, *England in the Twentieth Century*, p. 82.

10 L.C.B. Seaman, *Post Victorian Britain 1920–1951*, Methuen & Co. Ltd., 1966, p. 180.

11 Lansbury, *My Life*, p. 272.

12 Taylor, *English History*, p. 305.

13 Ibid., pp. 311–12.

14 Lansbury, *My Life*, pp. 280–81.

15 M. Foot, *Aneurin Bevan*, vol. 1, Paladin Granada, 1975, p. 101.

16 G. Brown, *Maxton*, Mainstream Publishing, 1986, p. 222.

17 G. Lansbury, *My England*, Selwyn and Blount Ltd., 1934, p. 228.

18 R. Postgate, *The Life of George Lansbury*, Longmans, Green & Co., 1951, p. 249.

19 M. Bondfield, *A Life's Work*, Hutchinson & Co., 1948, p. 297.

20 O. Mosley, *My Life*, Nelson, 1968, p. 254.

21 Taylor, *English History*, p. 359.

22 Mosley, *My Life*, p. 222.

23 Seaman, *Post Victorian Britain*, p. 212.

24 Morgan, *J. Ramsey MacDonald*, p. 197.

25 Cited in D. Thomson, *England in the Twentieth Century*, p. 106.

26 Marjorie Pinhorn, letter to the author. Mrs Pinhorn was a friend of Grace and Jessie Lansbury.

27 Lansbury, *My Life*, p. 285.

8

LEADER OF THE LABOUR PARTY

'No coup in the long history of constitutional government in England can have been quite as sensational as this,' wrote Margaret Bondfield of MacDonald's action.[1] Only fifteen Labour MPs followed MacDonald, leaving behind a Labour Party shocked by the desertion of the man who had spent much of his life working with them for the promotion of socialism. The parliamentary Labour Party elected the dependable Arthur Henderson as leader and settled down to oppose the National Government.

Snowden presented an emergency budget which increased income tax, cut the salaries of all public employees by at least 10 per cent, reduced unemployment benefit by 10 per cent and simultaneously limited benefit entitlement to twenty-six weeks in a year. The bankers duly provided credit of £80 million. However, the run on the pound continued and in September 1931 the Commons agreed to the very action which Snowden had previously said would be disastrous — Britain came off the gold standard. The value of the pound fell and then steadied. MacDonald then dissolved parliament.

MacDonald's move was an astute one. In the election campaign of October 1931, he and his colleagues were depicted as the people prepared to meet the crisis, the Labour Party as those who backed away. Moreover, in many constituencies Conservatives and Liberals did not stand against each other, so all their votes went to the single candidate prepared to support a National Government. The result was a landslide victory for the latter. Parties supporting the National Government had 521 seats, made up of 35 National Liberals, 13 National Labour and, the real victors, 473 Conservatives. The Labour Party, with a third of the vote, was decimated to 52 seats.

Henderson had lost his seat. The Labour Party needed a new leader and it chose Lansbury. Later he declared modestly, 'I owed my election as leader to no other reason than the fact that I was the only Labour Cabinet Minister who survived the Labour defeat of October, 1931.'[2] But there was more to it than that. A.J.P. Taylor writes that he:

> was the obvious choice as leader . . . His humble position as first commissioner of works did not represent his real standing in the Labour movement. He had long been a national figure, who could command audiences as big as MacDonald's and would have been a member of Labour's Big Four or Big Five if it had not been for MacDonald's dislike of him . . . As the hero of Poplarism, he had a unique skill in local government and was, in his own way, a master of parliamentary tactics.[3]

So the man who started by heaving coal on his back, who once left Britain to find work, who gave up the promise of a safe Liberal seat rather than compromise himself, who polled less than 400 votes in one election, who stood for parliament before there was a Labour Party, became the leader of His Majesty's Opposition. He was old and inexperienced in parliamentary leadership. Yet this was certain: he could be trusted. In him, the Labour Party knew that they had a leader who would never be seduced by the love of power, by the company of the establishment, by financial advantage. Raymond Postgate, who felt the pulse of the party, stated:

> The Party did not want another Olympian autocrat, or a Parliamentarian who could slur over difficulties by wordy formulas; it was reeling from the double shock of treachery and defeat. It wanted someone who could restore its confidence in human decency and its belief in its future.[4]

Lansbury was that man.

The task facing Lansbury was a daunting one. The parliamentary Labour Party had lost nearly all its major figures through desertion or electoral defeat. The size of some of the defeats — Hugh Dalton had a 8,203 majority overturned in the mining constituency of Bishop Auckland — reduced morale to rock bottom. Even amongst the remaining Labour MPs, relations were strained with the ILP members who considered that the Labour Party was losing its socialism. The links were finally cut in 1932.

Lansbury's priority was to take charge of and mould an opposition. Aided, in particular, by Clem Attlee and Stafford Cripps he spent endless hours in the Commons, arranging speakers for every debate, briefing them, encouraging them. They opposed the government when, in 1932, it imposed tariffs on many imported goods. They attacked the initial cuts not just in unemployment benefit but in public works schemes and school building. Lansbury himself led many of the opposition charges, repeatedly questioning ministers, always speaking for working-class people and at every opportunity raising issues of principle. The Labour Party responded to him and Postgate, who witnessed it, wrote:

> In Lansbury they found not only someone whom they loved and who loved them with no touch of patronage, but also a man who would repeat, in his full, hoarse voice, disregarding sniggers in the House of Commons and elsewhere, the truths about justice, kindness and equality that they wanted to hear again.[5]

Of all the topics that came before parliament, Lansbury was most concerned about those of unemployment and poverty. Neville Chamberlain, who soon took over from Snowden as chancellor of the exchequer, liked to indicate that such problems were fading as Britain entered an era of prosperity. He pointed to the increase in British production, to the boom in private housing, to the wide range of consumer goods, including radios and cars, which were purchased. He restored the cuts made by Snowden in public salaries and unemployment benefit. But Lansbury tore aside the complacency and identified the growing emergence of two nations, the affluent and the deprived, and expressed Labour's anger that the latter were not receiving a fair share of the nation's abundance. The unemployed still numbered nearly two million, and they were concentrated mainly in north-east England, South Wales and Scotland. The parliamentary front bench Labour spokesmen drew upon medical surveys to depict the poor nutrition, ill-health and inadequate housing of those who lived in poverty. Lansbury also turned to the churches and, in a letter to *The Times* of 11 October 1932, appealed to Christians to use their voice on behalf of the unemployed and the socially deprived.

Outside parliament, other forms of protest against unemployment were in full swing. The National Unemployed Workers' Movement organized large-scale marches, particularly in 1932 and 1934, which alarmed the government. Its communist leaders were put under close surveillance and some arrested. Two organizers, Tom Mann and Emrhys Llewellyn, were required by court to give sureties that no disorder would occur on a demonstration. On their refusal, they were jailed. Lansbury took up their case in the Commons where he argued that, as it was impossible for them to guarantee the future behaviour of others whom they might not even know, it constituted a serious breach of civil liberties. The home secretary had no adequate replies and no similar action was pursued against other organizers.

Shaken by the ferocity of the protests, the government took half-hearted action in two ways. In 1934, its Special Areas Act allowed the appointment of two commissioners, equipped with £2 million, to revive the depressed areas of Tyneside, West Cumberland, South Wales and Scotland. Lansbury welcomed direct government intervention but, with others, pointed out that the financial amount was pitiful when places such as Jarrow had unemployment rates of 67.8 per cent. Later the commissioners were given powers to start industrial estates but their overall effect on unemployment was minimal.

Next came the Unemployment Act of 1934. Chamberlain was keen to tidy up responsibility for unemployment and to further reduce the powers of local authorities. Workless people whose rights to insurance benefits had expired had become the responsibility of local authority public assistance committees which, in the eyes of many Conservatives, were treating them far too generously. Under the new act, the insurance system was continued, although under a new statutory committee. The main change was that responsibility for the unemployed whose insurance benefits had run out (or never existed) was placed with the Unemployment Assistance Board (UAB), a central body which would organize a uniform system throughout the country. The public assistance committees were left with the residue of other poor people.

Lansbury, as mentioned in a previous chapter, believed that only central government possessed the financial resources to fund adequately any system for supporting unemployed people. However, he perceived the limitations of the new scheme. One was that the semi-autonomous UAB was not responsible to ministers, unlike usual government departments. Indeed, MPs could not raise the cases of aggrieved constituents in the Commons. He saw this as a restriction on the powers of elected members. Another limitation concerned the difficulties of those unemployed persons who ran out of their insurance entitlement. Under the new scheme they still faced a considerable drop in income. The only change was that their fate had been transferred to another agency. Yet another fault was that UAB help was to be granted only after a rigid means test, renamed 'household needs test', which humiliated and demeaned applicants and, as under the Poor Law, would deter some from applying. Criticisms of this kind were hammered home in the Commons as Labour MP after Labour MP, with Stafford Cripps and Aneurin Bevan outstanding, rose to denounce the proposals. Even their fury was outdone by the reaction of the unemployed themselves once the UAB regulations, due to be effective in 1935, were made public. These revealed not only the extent of the all-pervasive means test — which, for instance, revealed that if the teenage son received a shilling a week extra at his job then that amount would be deducted from his father's dole money — but also that benefit levels would often be lower than those previously allowed by public assistance committees. Bill Moore has written a graphic account of the protests in Sheffield where a demonstration of over 30,000 led to struggles with and arrests by the police.[6] Similar massive turnouts, often organized by the NUWM, took place at Glasgow, Pontypridd and Aberdare and many other areas of high unemployment. So widespread were the protests that the government had to postpone the introduction of the regulations for further consideration and could not bring them back until a much later date. Michael Foot called this 'the biggest single Labour victory of the thirties' and continued:

> The deed had been done by a combined operation; by deadly parliamentary manoeuvre and attack in the face of vastly superior numbers, with the infantry from the back benches let loose in support of Cripp's cavalry charges; and, more important still, by the mobilization and unleashing of a united working class, marching and demonstrating on the streets.[7]

Any sense of political satisfaction derived by Lansbury from the stout performances of the Labour opposition was marred by the greatest loss of his life. On 23 March 1933, Bessie died, aged seventy-two. Bessie never wrote about herself and it is fortunate that a book by son Edgar, published a year later, gives some glimpses of her character. Bessie was an East End character in her own right, one who worked for a number of local organizations. Such activity was the more remarkable because Bessie also gave herself wholeheartedly to the well-being of her large family. As Edgar recalls, the weekly wash in the Lansbury household was like a laundry industry. Yet not only did Bessie cope adequately and lovingly with her own children; she sometimes also made room for others who were in desperate need and later gave much time to her grandchildren. Edgar also told of the happy relationship between Bessie and George. Of course there were occasional differences, but they were soon rectified. Bessie was devoted to what Edgar calls 'the Cause' and so accepted the hours, energy and money which George put into advancing socialism. In the last years of her life, with all the children grown up, Bessie and George spent more time together. They even went to the cinema and theatre, which they had never done in their younger days, as well as enjoying that memorable trip to Russia. Edgar wrote, 'During those years I know that they made up to each other in love, companionship and happiness much that had been sacrificed earlier in their lives for the Cause.'[8]

Tributes to Bessie poured in from many quarters: from Christians, Jews and Buddhists: from working-class organizations in the West Indies and from Gandhi in India: from shopkeepers and fairground workers; and, of course, from numerous relatives, neighbours and political friends. George preserved all the letters but could say little. He was emotionally and physically overcome by the loss of the woman whom he had loved and who had loved him for over fifty years. Not until later could he pen his feelings when he wrote that Bessie:

> exercised an influence over my life which no words of mine will ever adequately express . . . both of us believed marriage was for eternity; and this, when the tide of tempers rose, or when adversity swept down, kept us young enough in heart to be able to say: 'No matter we still have each other; let's forget everything else.'[9]

Shaken though he was, Lansbury returned to the political fray. As well as leading the party in the Commons, he toured the country addressing scores of meetings as he attempted to revive Labour's fortunes. George Thomas, later a Labour MP, speaker of the House of Commons and then Lord Tonypandy, was then a young Labour activist in South Wales. He once invited Lansbury to speak to the Workers' Temperance League, which was allied to the Labour Party. To his surprise, the Labour leader accepted. He said:

> Lansbury, leader of the party, could take time out to come down to that little valley. I doubt if we were able to pay his fare. He certainly wouldn't have had a fee. But he knew that drink played a terrible part in working-class life and caused family problems and therefore, whether popular or unpopular, he came out against it quite openly.'

Thomas was delighted at a turnout of over 300, including all the local MPs. Wherever he went, Lansbury drew large crowds as he proclaimed the socialist gospel. He won new members and inspired existing ones to renew their vision that Labour would become the government of Britain.

Lansbury was working flat out. He seemed to welcome speaking engagements, which filled his life without Bessie. He possessed a strong physique and constitution but he was seventy-four and the inevitable happened on 9 December 1933. Having opened a bazaar at Gainsborough Town Hall, he was proceeding to a socialist meeting when he tripped over a step and broke a thigh. Despite his great pain, he called out, 'This is only an incident. Carry on with the meeting.' For some days fears were expressed for his life, but he pulled round and took an enforced rest until July 1933.

The long stay in hospital proved important to Lansbury. It reassured him that he had the affection and support of many in the country. *The Times* of 11 December, after reporting that the king had conveyed his best wishes, added:

> Although Mr Lansbury is one of the least compromising of protagonists in debate, he has never failed to hold the liking and respect of a House that is overwhelmingly hostile to his opinions.

If *The Times*, so often critical of Lansbury, showed its respect for him, so much more did socialists of all kinds. Postgate wrote about the hundreds of letters he received that 'most were from supporters, women and men whose only object was to tell him that they admired and loved him, and needed him'.[10] One unsigned letter spoke for many in saying that:

it's just because you don't know me that I'm writing to you, just to thank you from the bottom of my heart for all that you have meant and done for me, with your great big hearted, inspiring conduct and expression of your life.

Lansbury had often been exposed to attacks from the other side in the Commons, from Conservative journalists, and even from socialists who considered him too extreme or too moderate. He knew that on recovery he would be back in the firing line. Meanwhile, the piles of messages, the visits, the plaudits, recharged his emotional batteries for what lay ahead.

The rest also gave him the time to write *My England*. Written in plain English, this book manages to be both straightforward and beautiful. It is idealistic in depicting Lansbury's vision of a socialist Britain yet practical in outlining the policies required to attain it. It is broad in a sweep that takes in world socialism yet narrow enough to portray socialism as a creed which shapes the behaviour of one individual to another. It is the book of a man who looks out of his Bow window and feels compassion for the unemployed he sees outside; of a man who experiences deep anger at the society that allows wealth for some and poverty for others; of a man who expresses his appreciation of ordinary socialist friends who will continue the struggle to abolish that poverty. This compassion, anger and appreciation all sprang from Lansbury's capacity to love. He loved the East End, loved England, loved children, loved the poorest and most oppressed of people. Unlike many politicians of his time — and later — Lansbury was not ashamed to talk about love and he boldly wrote:

I want a new England to be crowded with such people — men and women full of the blessed spirit of love and friendship.[11]

He possessed that spirit and it vibrates from every page in this, his most complete, most moving and most compelling book.

Additionally, the illness afforded Lansbury the opportunity to reflect upon his spiritual position. He emerged stronger in his Christian beliefs. He declared:

In the very earliest, darkest hours of illness I was not afraid of what would befall me; I had no dread of God as my Father and my Judge.[12]

His faith remained firm on the Christ, of whom he liked to read in the Gospels. When on earth, this Jesus 'spent His time doing good. He lived among people sharing their lives.'[13] This goodness and sharing, he re-affirmed, could only be maximized in a socialist society. He thus stated in *My England*:

> My reading and my prayers have all united to confirm my faith that Socialism, which means love, co-operation, and brotherhood in every department of human affairs, is the only outward expression of a Christian faith.'[14]

George's faith convinced him that he would be reunited with Bessie in eternal life. His convictions were soon to be needed again for, in 1935, Edgar died of cancer aged forty-eight. Edgar, probably the son closest to George, had followed in his political footsteps both as a Guardian and Labour councillor. More, as Edgar's book revealed, they were close emotionally, in almost daily contact, supporting and loving each other in good and bad times. Now, with Edgar gone, daughter Annie became even more than a daughter. She kept house for him, cooked the meals and demonstrated that practical closeness which was a feature of Lansbury family life.

As A.J.P. Taylor explains, Lansbury was the ideal leader for Labour while economic affairs were predominant but, 'Things were different when international affairs took the centre of the stage.'[15] He returned from his long illness committed not just to socialism but also to pacifism. This belief did not create divisions with regard to India. Following the Government of India Act of 1935, Lansbury spoke in the Commons and made a radio broadcast in which he criticized the legislation for not granting full independence. In this, he had the full backing of the party. But his pacifism was not shared by an increasing number of socialists and this difference became both important and problematic as events in Europe made armed conflict a possibility once more.

In January 1933, Adolf Hitler became chancellor of Germany. Within a few months, Germany withdrew both from a major disarmament conference and from the League of Nations. The fact of German re-armament and the prospect of another war had to be faced. Many were prepared to oppose Germany by force again. For others, the memories of the horrors of the 1914–18 war drove them to support the Peace Pledge Union. In February 1933, the

Oxford University Union held its famous debate and carried the motion 'That this House will in no circumstances fight for its King and Country'. Then, in October 1933, a pacifist Labour candidate won a by-election at East Fulham by overturning a National Government majority of 14,000. Despite this victory, the Labour party was by no means wholly pacifist. Indeed, a strong and growing wing argued that eventually Britain would have to take up arms against Fascism. Lansbury was thus in a difficult position. He was a well-known pacifist yet, as leader, he had to recognize that his views did not represent many in the party. He supported the League of Nations as an arbitrator of international disputes and opposed British rearmament. However, awkward questions then arose. What would he do if the League needed to take armed intervention to stop a hostile power or if it became clear that Britain was to be attacked? Lansbury, in some difficulties, replied that he favoured general not unilateral disarmament and recognized — even if it was not his view — that Britain would require sufficient arms to defend itself.

In the middle of 1934, Lansbury faced a deteriorating international scene. A government White Paper of March 1935 then indicated that Britain would rely on armed force rather than on collective security and so opened the door to rearmament. Hitler immediately restored conscription in Germany, while Italy was poised to invade Abyssinia, a fellow member of the League of Nations. In September, Lansbury attended the TUC annual conference, where most delegates indicated that they would support the League of Nations if it decided to take economic and military sanctions against Italy. Not being in agreement, Lansbury made an uncomfortable speech in which he denounced war without repudiating the TUC position. He now considered resigning as leader but close colleagues persuaded him to stay on. They knew a general election was in the offing and did not want to face it without Lansbury at the helm.

The Labour Party conference followed in October 1935 at Brighton. Lansbury perceived that Labour opinion was swinging towards that of the TUC, ably expressed by Ernie Bevin, that pacifism and disarmament would only help the advance of Fascist dictators. He again tried to resign, but again his colleagues persuaded him otherwise. Italian troops were now in Abyssinia and Hugh Dalton, for the Labour Party Executive, moved a resolution which urged the government to call upon the League of Nations to stop the Italians by any necessary measures. A full debate ensued with Stafford Cripps opposing the motion but with most supporting the case put by Clem Attlee that intervention here might stop the spread of war elsewhere.

When Lansbury rose, he received a tremendous ovation. As Taylor put it, he 'was loved as no Labour leader had been since Keir Hardie'.[16] He immediately acknowledged that his views were at variance with the majority and hinted he would resign. Cries of 'No, no,' filled the hall. Visibly affected, Lansbury proceeded to make probably the most moving speech of his long political life, of which just a few extracts can be presented.

> I have gone into mining areas, I have gone into my own district when people have been starving or semi-starving; I have stood in the midst of dockers who have been on the verge of starvation . . . and I have said to them: 'No, you must not rise, you must have no violence, you must trust to the winning of this through public opinion.' I have never at any time said to workers of this country: 'You must take up either arms, or sticks, or stones, in order to force your way to the end that you seek to attain.' And when I am challenged on all these issues, I say to myself this: I have no right to preach pacifism to starving people in this country and preach something else in relation to people elsewhere . . . I have said it in Russia when my Russian comrades allowed me to see a review of their air force, and when they took me on one of their warships. I have never under any circumstances said that I believed you could obtain Socialism by force.
>
> And why have I said that? I have said it, first, because One whose life I revere and who, I believe, is the greatest Figure in history, has put it on record: 'Those who take the sword shall perish by the sword.'
>
> It may be that I shall not meet you on this platform any more. (cries of 'No') There are things that come into life that make changes inevitable. It may very well be that in the carrying out of your policy I shall be in your way. When I was sick and on my back ideas came into my head, and one was that the only thing worth while for old men to do is to at least say the thing they believe, and to at least try to warn the young of the dangers of force and compulsion . . . If mine was the only voice at this conference, I would say in the name of the faith I hold, the belief

I have that God intended us to live peaceably and quietly with one another, that if some people do not allow us to do so, I am ready to stand as the early Christians did, and say, 'This is our faith, this is where we stand, and, if necessary, this is where we will die.'

Lansbury's noble address was followed by an ignoble one from Bevin. He sneered at Lansbury for hawking 'your conscience round from body to body asking to be told what to do with it'. He accused him of hypocrisy in now opposing sanctions while having previously approved of a pamphlet, *Socialism and Peace*, which advocated them. Lansbury was disappointed that no Labour leader rose to say that they had refused to accept his resignation and annoyed that Bevin had overlooked the fact that he, Lansbury, had been in hospital when the pamphlet was issued. Despite some protests about the tone of Bevin's speech, the resolution was carried by a large majority. A few days later, Lansbury again offered his resignation to the Labour MPs. Once more they refused to accept it by thirty-eight votes to seven with five abstaining. But this time he insisted and they reluctantly agreed. Subsequently, they appointed Attlee in his place.

Stanley Baldwin, who had taken over from the ailing MacDonald as prime minister, then took the opportunity to call a general election. The outcome was National Government supporters 432 seats, Labour 154 and Liberals 20. Labour had made gains but nothing like as great as their expectations. Undoubtedly they missed Lansbury's leadership, and Michael Foot blames Bevin for forcing him out, saying, 'Ernie Bevin didn't have any reckoning of what were going to be the consequences . . . and he didn't really care very much.' Lansbury, incidentally, with an election address which called for expenditure on nursery schools, better wages and pensions, houses and jobs rather than on guns and poisonous gas, obtained a result bettered by few others. He won by 19,064 to 5,707 votes. As for the National Government, despite Baldwin's words it did nothing to help Abyssinia and the discredited League of Nations came almost to an end.

In his day, the respect for Lansbury's leadership was revealed not just in the great ovations he received at meetings. On his resignation, the *Daily Herald* of 15 November 1935 praised his achievements and called him 'not only the most loved figure in the Labour movement, but perhaps in the whole of politics'. His successor, Clem Attlee, never one given to fulsome praise, recorded his thanks for Lansbury's integrity and 'very able leadership'.[17]

Today, however, Lansbury's role in the years 1931–35 is often ignored in histories of the period or dismissed with passing and often negative references. Thus L.C.B. Seaman, in his textbook, writes him off as 'politically illiterate'[18] while Henry Pelling in his Labour history asserts that:

> the Parliamentary Labour Party was a poor and nerveless thing in the Parliament of the early 1930s. Lansbury himself was already 72, and was in any case a poor leader because of his tendency to woolly-minded sentimentality.[19]

These judgments are so far removed from those of contemporaries of Lansbury that an explanation must be sought. Michael Foot, a participant in the events of this era, often spoke to and listened to Lansbury and his parliamentary team. In his widely acclaimed biography of Aneurin Bevan, Foot argues that certain writers have misjudged the Labour history of this period because they have relied too heavily on the writings and perspectives of Ernie Bevin and Hugh Dalton. He states:

> An entirely false picture has been painted of Labour's role in the 1931–35 Parliament, largely owing to an uncritical acceptance of the views of the two chief leaders of the movement outside the Commons, Bevin and Dalton.[20]

Bevin and Dalton were not sympathetic to Lansbury's insistence on socialist morality and principle rather than on what they termed as 'realism'. And neither agreed with his pacifism. Indeed Dalton had fought in the First World War and Bevin was later to become a minister in Churchill's war cabinet during the Second World War. Foot also asserts that Dalton, in his diaries, played down the importance of these years because he was out of the Commons from 1931 to 1935 and wanted to focus attention on the subsequent period when he regained his seat.

Foot's own recent assessment of Lansbury given in an interview with the author, was that he:

> was a very fine leader of the party after 1931. . . . One of the reasons why the party recovered after 1931 and why its spirit

recovered despite the fact of the appalling defeat was the spirit which Lansbury showed.

And elsewhere he wrote that:

> the rebuilding of the Party after the 1931 catastrophe was heroic; a combined feat of idealism and pragmatism, and George Lansbury was its embodiment.[21]

Lansbury's parliamentary colleagues, especially Cripps and Attlee, valued his leadership so much that they consistently tried to persuade him to continue. Outside the Commons, George Thomas reflected the views of many Labour activists in his deep appreciation of what Lansbury did for the party. Even political opponents such as Baldwin acknowledged his achievements. It is fair, therefore, to claim that Lansbury made three significant contributions as leader of the Labour Party.

First, after the crushing defeat of 1931, he ensured that there was an organized opposition at all. Against a government of over 500, Lansbury had a handful of MPs and even they were not united. They included some who had gone along with MacDonald's cautious approach, some who saw themselves mainly as trade unionists, and the few ILPers. The latter eventually left the party but the formation of the Socialist League ensured a base for left wingers who pressed the party to give up any ideas of Fabian gradualism. The one unifying factor was that they all held Lansbury in high regard and he used this allegiance to mould them into a team which questioned, harried and opposed the government with an effectiveness out of all proportion to its numbers. Lansbury gave particular attention to developing the parliamentary skills of Cripps and Attlee, who were the favourites to succeed him. Michael Foot wrote:

> It was probably the happiest collaboration that Labour had ever known at the top, and the example of full-scale aggression against the Tories helped to induce a spirit of comradeship along the back benches.[22]

Consequently, the backbenchers became noted — not for their sniping at their own leaders, as sometimes happens in Labour circles — but for the role they played in parliamentary debates against the National Government. Thus young Aneurin Bevan found many opportunities to sharpen his debating skills to the cost of his opponents and to the delight of Lansbury.

Lansbury also succeeded in restoring the shattered morale of the Labour Party. Initially, he did so within the Commons. From observing him, Michael Foot concluded, 'Lansbury was sharp minded and could express himself forcibly. He knew what the political enemy was and he would attack with great force and skill.' He feared no one and, at times, took on, verbally duelled with and overcame Winston Churchill who, although out of the cabinet, was regarded as *the* enemy of the working class by many socialists. Lansbury also showed a capacity for mastering detail. For instance, during the debate on the Coal Mines Bill in June 1932, he noticed that the government, in declaring that it would continue the seven-and-a-half hour day, was blurring over the subject of miners' wages. He then continually pressed the government spokesman until he clarified the legal obligations about raising them. But detail was second to principle. Lansbury took every chance to talk about equality, justice and co-operation. He repeatedly and powerfully put across his view that, under a Labour administration, Britain would be a fairer and happier society. To quote again from Michael Foot's interview with the author, 'He led that small team against the great mass of government . . . and on some occasions he was able to stir the country.' Out in the country, ordinary socialists such as George Thomas had felt completely dejected by the betrayal of MacDonald and the crushing electoral defeat. Their faith was restored when they read of Lansbury's performances and, in some cases, when they heard him themselves. Thomas said, 'He not only saved the soul of the party, he saved the party. We could have sunk into oblivion and the Liberals could have been reborn because there's got to be an opposition.' It was Lansbury who ensured that Labour was that opposition and that it was a skilled and vibrant one.

Outside the Commons, as well, Lansbury did not spare himself. He spoke at meetings all over Britain with an energy and dedication that would have done credit to a man half his age. He even found time for writing and broadcasting. And in every sphere he conveyed his love for humanity and his belief that socialism was the faith and system most likely to promote a better world. No wonder that wherever he went he was greeted by crowds of appreciative supporters. In the early 1930s, Lansbury represented socialism more than any other person in Britain and hence people wanted to see and hear him for themselves. When they did, they usually left feeling uplifted by his vision of the part they could play in building a socialist society.

The revival of the Labour Party's morale was reflected in some electoral successes. The notable by-election victory at East Fulham has already been mentioned. In the same year of 1933, Labour gained control of over 200 boroughs in local elections. The following year, it won control of the London County Council for the first time. Of course, such successes are not attributable to Lansbury alone. Within parliament, other MPs performed ably and bravely. The establishment of the Labour Party machinery in London owed most to Herbert Morrison. Labour Party policies and documents were being hammered out by people such as Hugh Dalton. Most of all, as Lansbury insisted on noting, countless and now unknown socialists worked for the party at all levels. Nonetheless, nearly all looked to him. They knew that he would never desert the Labour Party. They knew that his socialism was a matter of deeds as well as words. They looked to him, knew him, and were inspired to strive again for socialism.

Finally, in his leadership of the Labour Party, Lansbury also did a service for democracy. At this time, democracy was being crushed in parts of Europe. Lansbury himself recorded of elected parliaments that 'these institutions are badly discredited and the ugly, brutal, soul-destroying force of dictatorships reigns supreme in many lands. Mussolini, Hitler and Pilsudski have all been accepted.'[23] In Britain, fascists were depicting the virtues of a one-party state while some saw the massive majority of the National Government as a step in that direction. If the remnant of the Labour Party had been split, ineffective and leaderless then that government would have had virtually no opposition. Fortunately, the opposite happened. The Labour Party held together and not only criticized government policies but also convinced the public that there were alternative policies and an alternative party at hand. Thus Stanley Baldwin praised the Labour opposition and the Lansbury leadership for having 'helped to keep the flag of Parliamentary government flying in the world'[24]

Perhaps the best and most surprising compliment to Lansbury's leadership came from A.J. Cummins. Cummins was the renowned political correspondent for the *News Chronicle* and both he and the paper were long-standing critics of the Labour Party. Moreover, Cummins wrote an assessment of Lansbury not as a tribute after he lost his position but while he still held it in January 1934. Initially, Cummins had considered that Lansbury's lack of experience in parliamentary tactics, his limited intellectual capacities, and the sheer enormity of the task of dealing with intricate and extensive legislation would result in him making 'a feeble showing as leader of a nearly non-existent Opposition'. Yet, after watching him closely and frequently in the Commons, Cummins had to revise his opinions. He wrote:

> His genuine moral sense, his passionate sincerity, his fine simplicity of mind which searches instinctively for the realities of any human issue, transcended any clumsiness of expression and broke down again and again the defences and pretences of simple-minded official spokesmen.
>
> He commands now not the fear but the respect and admiration of the House of Commons. He has given new life and a new home to his Party inside and outside the House. . . . He has done more than any other person in the British Isles to create and consolidate a new opposition to Toryism and to renew the faith of millions in a constitutional alternative.

References

1   M. Bondfield, *A Life's Work*, Hutchinson & Co., 1948, p. 304.

2   G. Lansbury, *My England*, Selwyn and Blount Ltd., 1934, p. 14.

3   A.J.P.Taylor, *English History 1914–1945*, Penguin Books, reprinted 1987, p. 408.

4   R. Postgate, *The Life of George Lansbury*, Longmans, Green & Co., 1951, p. 277.

5   Ibid., p. 277.

6   B. Moore, *All Out*, Sheffield City Libraries, 1985.

7   M. Foot, *Aneurin Bevan*, vol. 1, Paladin Granada, 1975, p. 207.

8   E. Lansbury, *George Lansbury, My Father*, Sampson Low, Marston & Co., 1934, p. 89.

9   Cited by Postgate, *Life of George Lansbury*, p. 21.

10   Ibid., p. 292.

[11] Lansbury, *My England*, p. 31.

[12] Ibid., p. 37.

[13] Ibid., p. 32.

[14] Ibid., p. 37.

[15] Taylor, *English History*, p. 408.

[16] Ibid., p. 470.

[17] C. Attlee, *The Labour Party in Perspective*, Victor Gollancz, 1937, p. 60.

[18] L.C.B. Seaman, *Post Victorian Britain 1920–1951*, Methuen & Co. Ltd., 1966, p. 212.

[19] Cited by Foot, *Aneurin Bevan*, note 8, p. 206.

[20] Ibid.

[21] M. Foot, 'Ideals and Raw Deals', *Guardian*, 10 April 1987.

[22] Foot, *Aneurin Bevan*, p. 167.

[23] Lansbury, *My England*, p. 21.

[24] Cited by Taylor, *English History*, p. 407.

9

THE LAST YEARS

Relieved of his position as leader, Lansbury took the opportunity to see more of his children and grandchildren. During these years, he was particularly close to son William who, according to his son Terry, had developed into 'a hard headed, hard drinking businessman'. His wife, Jessie, was an alcoholic who made several suicide attempts and this led him to take an action which caused George some pain — he sent young Terry to boarding school. This difference, however, never endangered the Lansbury ties. According to Terry, 'GL was wonderfully kind and understanding towards mother's weakness (or illness) and always tried to comfort her with love . . . never a reproach.'[1] Now George relied heavily on William for transport and some financial support, which he sometimes used to succour those who daily knocked on his door.

It was not just William. He had warm feelings for all his relatives. He was proud of daughter Dorothy when she became mayor of Shoreditch. He followed with some amusement the theatrical career of granddaughter Daphne, another child of William and Jessie, as she appeared in London revues and pantomimes. Edgar's daughter Angela was also showing signs of interest in the stage. After all, her mother, Moyna McGill, had been a prominent actress. George also saw much of Daisy and her husband Raymond and the latter retained a deep affection and respect for him despite some political disagreements over foreign policy. In addition, Violet had returned from Russia where she left her two sons in the care of her in-laws. Violet considered that the two boys would not have adapted to Britain. Not least, George leaned heavily on his devoted Annie.

The Lansburys always held a family gathering at Christmas. While Bessie was alive, it was held at 39 Bow Road where Terry recalls George as 'a wonderfully warm person who would sit us all on his knee in turn, a warm pink presence with prickly white whiskers, a lovely puppy fresh smell and a deep crackly voice saying "Cheerio young fellow me lad" whether one was a boy or girl grandchild'.[2] After Bessie's death, Daisy and Raymond Postgate held the Christmas celebration at their home in Finchley. Another grandson, John Postgate, enjoyed the annual parties but added:

> As I grew older I learned of tremendous tensions among the parents at these gatherings: Violet, virulent communist, had to be kept out of the way of Dolly and Ray; Annie, Christian fundamentalist, was only on speaking terms with Nellie; Ernest, rather right-wing Labour MP for Shoreditch and Dolly's husband, was regarded by some as a traitor to the Cause; these and other antagonisms in the first generation of his strong-minded offspring were amazing and persisted long after his death. But his pleasure in assembling his descendants outweighed such relative trivialities.[3]

Even in his old age, however, family life was never sufficient for George Lansbury. He accepted numerous official engagements in Poplar and addressed many meetings outside. He travelled much abroad, and he continued to write articles and books. When Raymond Postgate started a monthly socialist journal called *Fact*, costing just sixpence, Lansbury became a contributing editor and, in October 1937, wrote one entitled *Why Pacifists Should Be Socialists*.

In the Commons, Lansbury continued to speak frequently. He advocated a forty-eight hour week for hospital staff and referred movingly to the care he had received. Nurses in the public gallery rose to cheer him and were ejected. The motion was defeated. He joined in any attack on unemployment and poverty and castigated the government for expecting an unemployed couple with three dependent children, and one earning 16 shillings a week, to survive on the £2-1s-6d awarded by the UAB. On 20 February 1939, *Hansard* records him saying:

> I know what it costs to bring up a child and I know what it costs to keep myself. I am just as virtuous or vicious as any man in this House. I do not smoke. I am a teetotaller. I hardly ever go to a play and I never go to the dogs, but I have not enough money.

His point was that if he found difficulties on the pay of an MP, how could families be expected to live on less.

For all his concern with poverty, Lansbury, like many others, was most worried about the deteriorating situation in Europe. In 1936, Hitler and Mussolini had forged the Rome–Berlin Axis and so paved the way for united Fascist aggression in the West. Then came the Spanish Civil War, in which Italy and Germany supplied arms to General Franco as he attempted to overthrow the elected Republican government. The National Government in Britain decided it had no right to invervene. The Labour Party was divided. Many believed that socialists would have to take an armed stand against Fascism and some bravely fought with the International Brigade in Spain. Others did not want to do anything which might ignite a European war and the Labour Party initially opposed intervention. Interestingly, Ernie Bevin, who had so castigated Lansbury for opposing sanctions, led the move against official intervention. Neville Chamberlain, who succeeded Baldwin as prime minister, continued the policy of what has been called 'appeasement' and refused calls for action when Japan resumed its invasion of China. None the less, by this time both the National Government and a majority within the Labour Party were convinced that war was inevitable and that rearmament was necessary. Lansbury now felt a growing distance between his pacifist views and those of many of his Labour colleagues. He decided he had to give more of his time to the cause of peace and, although he continued to speak on foreign policy issues in the Commons, he devoted more and more effort to activities outside.

Lansbury wrote:

> After the General Election I went from one end of Britain to the other in company with my pacifist comrades of the Fellowship of Reconciliation, Peace Pledge Union, Women's Co-operative Guild, and many Labour and religious organisations, speaking on behalf of the gospel of Pacifism.[4]

The Fellowship of Reconciliation consisted mainly of Quakers and other non-conformists and Lansbury, as Ceadle notes in his history of pacifism, was 'a rare representative both of the Labour movement and of Anglicanism'.[5] The best known peace agency, however, was the Peace Pledge Union (PPU).

In her account of the PPU, Sybil Morrison named Lansbury

as one of its founders in 1934 along with such people as Ellen Wilkinson, Arthur Ponsonby, Charles Raven, Siegfried Sassoon and Dick Sheppard.[6] The moving spirit was undoubtedly the Rev. Dick Sheppard who galvanized others into action and who created an organization which, by 1936, had over 100,000 members pledged not to fight and looking to unilateral disarmament as the means of avoiding war.

Lansbury's contribution was significant. He was the PPU's most noted speaker. In August 1935, his famous 'Truce of God' letter to *The Times* had urged Christians, and members of other faiths, to meet in Jerusalem and 'from Mount Calvary call a Truce of God and bid the war spirit rest'. Sheppard perceived Lansbury's capacity to touch human chords and immediately organized a meeting at Central Hall, Westminster. Four thousand people crowded in while hundreds were locked out. In like manner, wherever Lansbury went, he attracted large crowds. Of course, not all were receptive. As war drew nearer he suffered accusations of supporting Britain's enemies. Bill Fishman recalls hearing him speak for pacifism at Bethnal Green Town Hall where abuse like 'Shut up you silly old Bible puncher' was hurled at him.[7] In a letter in the Lansbury Collection, Mrs Ursula Roberts describes a meeting in Bournemouth where a pro-war speaker was loudly cheered while Lansbury's plea for peace was met with jeers. She wrote, 'No one spoke to G.L. when the meeting broke up. I edged my way towards him and thanked him. It was obvious as he replied that he was sick at heart.'

Lansbury could accept such hostility, for he knew that he did make positive impressions on many listeners. The Rev. Donald Soper, then a young Methodist minister, first met him at a PPU meeting in Leicester. In an interview with the author, Soper said:

> I can remember vividly the impression he made on me at first sight. He was bulky, large, he sprawled . . . I warmed to him. He was very gracious to me. He had never heard of me. His speaking voice was common, there was no quality about it, it was a very flat voice. But he had this inner sense of conviction and solidarity of mind which was impressive from the very first sentence that he uttered. He was not nimble-witted but he knew what he wanted to say and in simple language he said it.

Similarly, he made a strong impact on Vera Brittain at a giant open-air meeting at Dorchester on 20 June 1936. She described the occasion as 'a turning point of my life', and she determined to follow the pacifism and the Christianity of Lansbury and Sheppard.[8] Lansbury thus played a major part in winning people to the cause of pacifism in general and to the PPU in particular. Indeed, the PPU grew into the largest peace body in Europe.

Lansbury also acted as the voice of pacifism in the Commons. Even when the Labour Party dropped its opposition to re-armament, Lansbury continued to argue that increased arms led to increased chances of war. On 8 March 1938, when speaking on an amendment to the government's White Paper on Defence, he read out the PPU manifesto which stressed that pacifism, as well as being about the refusal to fight, was a policy based on economic appeasement and the establishment of a new League of Nations.

For a while, the PPU won widespread support and became an influential force within Britain. But in October 1937, it lost its main leader when Dick Sheppard died. A number of Labour MPs, such as Ellen Wilkinson and Reginald Jorenson, withdrew as they concluded that Britain would have to defend itself against Fascism. Lansbury took over as president but, by the end of the decade, membership numbers had dropped. Donald Soper concluded that its failure was because it was:

> too remote from political action. Dick Sheppard invested the whole affair with a kind of chivalry and gallantry. It was almost a crusade rather than a political movement. In my judgement, it was the failure to relate the pacifist commitment to a political environment which could sustain it which caused the defection of people.

Soper then went on to make the intriguing comment:

> I fell very much under the spell of Dick Sheppard but, looking back, far from Lansbury being the fool and Sheppard the inspired leader, it was probably the other way round.

Whatever the reasons, the PPU failed to influence official British foreign policy or policy over rearmament. Moreover, it failed to persuade a mass movement to refuse to join the armed forces. At least, it could claim that the Second World War saw far more conscientious objectors than the First World War. Further, the PPU survived the war. Its paper, *Peace News*, continued to circulate and a small pacifist influence was maintained within both the Labour Party and the churches. Later, the movement expanded again with the cause of nuclear disarmament. Some credit should be given to George Lansbury for the establishment and survival of the PPU.

In 1936, the US Emergency Peace Campaign invited Lansbury to tour the United States. Accompanied by his daughter, Daisy, and by fellow MP and Christian Dr Arthur Salter, Lansbury met President Franklin Roosevelt and spoke in twenty-six cities within six weeks — and he was now aged seventy-seven. His speaking abilities, his personal attributes and his devotion to the cause of peace made a strong impression on Dr Salter. His biographer, Fenner Brockway, wrote:

> Salter always had unbounded admiration for Lansbury. Now his feeling approached hero-worship. 'GL is doing more for real peace than all the official politicians of all the camps put together', he exclaimed.[9]

The success of the tour gave Lansbury the idea of his future role. He knew that the horrors of war were near. He acknowledged that many in his own party were now ready to support war. Indeed, Ben Pimlott, in his biography of Dalton, points out that the Labour Party which was essentially against rearmament and armed intervention in 1933 was, by 1937, 'a party that believed in armed deterrence . . . that bitterly opposed Neville Chamberlain's policy of appeasement'.[10] Lansbury's response was that individuals like himself would have to promote international peace. He was not thinking of mere summit meetings to exchange pleasantries with world leaders. His socialist analysis was that the major cause of war was rooted in economic inequality and competition. He saw that some countries were denied markets and materials which they therefore sought by conquest. He also believed that mass unemployment created unrest which found an outlet in either internal or external violence. Ultimately, he reckoned that peace would only be lasting in a socialist world where nations co-operated in free trade. In the meantime, he looked for an economic peace conference which would result in investment in needy countries, stabilized currencies, lower tariffs and increased sharing of materials and markets.

Lansbury's thinking coincided with that of the Embassies of Reconciliation, a small committee which included Canon Raven and Barrow Cadbury, whose objective was to send men and women to points of conflict in order to mediate for peace. The committee supported Lansbury and in August 1936 he visited the French premier Léon Blum and later made trips to Belgium, Denmark, Norway and Sweden. Speaking in the Commons, on his return, of the desires of these nations for peace and an economic conference, Lansbury met some heckling and shouts of 'Go and tell that to Hitler.' To their surprise, he did just that and met Hitler in Berlin on 19 April 1937. They spoke, through interpreters, for two-and-a-quarter hours.

In his book, *My Quest for Peace*, Lansbury commented, 'I think history will record Herr Hitler as one of the great men of our time.'[11] This did not mean that he admired Hitler, for he also recorded that he was a 'fanatic' who countenanced murders and concentration camps. It was rather an acknowledgment that Hitler had won the backing of many if not most German people by bringing order out of chaos and by restoring national pride. During the interview, Hitler listed his achievements. Lansbury spoke to him about Christianity and protested at the Nazi persecution of Jews, Christians and political nonconformists — a few of whom were subsequently released. He then moved on to the main purpose of the visit: to seek Hitler's support 'for the proposed new world conference to deal with the economic and financial causes of war'.[12]

Following the interview, a newspaper offered Lansbury a large sum for an exclusive account — an early attempt at cheque-book journalism. He declined and issued a statement to all in which he said that Hitler desired peace with France, that he was prepared to reduce armaments if Britain and France did the same, and that he would attend a conference if organized by President Roosevelt or some other great leader.

From Germany, Lansbury went on to Denmark to chair the War Resisters' International conference which supported conscientious objectors, to Italy to speak to Mussolini, to Czechoslovakia, Poland and Austria. In Vienna, the last words of his address to the nation's politicians were a plea to 'kneel to Jesus Christ . . . to reject violence and accept the way of love, become citizens of the Kingdom of Heaven.'[13]

All was in vain. In March 1938, Hitler annexed Austria. In September, Chamberlain had his famous Munich meeting with

Hitler and returned saying that Hitler would be satisfied if Czech Germans came under German rule and that he did not want war with Britain. His words were enthusiastically welcomed by both the National Government and the Labour opposition. But both nations continued to arm and, in March 1939, Hitler invaded Czechoslovakia. As war became more imminent, so Lansbury's trips became the butt of both scorn and criticism. Emmanuel Shinwell sneered at 'the lampooning in the world's press of Lansbury, the roving ambassador determined to prove that no human being was wholly evil and no nation deaf to an uplifting message'.[14] He was attacked for not seeing the evils of Germany and for being taken in by Hitler. He was ridiculed for thinking that disarmament and conferences might bring about peace. Some even made unkind remarks about the effects of old age on his brain. Postgate comments that his mission to Europe was 'mostly responsible for Lansbury's reputation as a man whose heart was stronger than his head'.[15]

One of these criticisms can easily be dismissed: Lansbury was not senile. In discussing the varied explanations of the Second World War, A.J.P. Taylor includes 'German grievances against the peace settlement of 1919 (and) failure to agree on a system of general controlled disarmament'.[16] Lansbury identified these danger points in the 1920s and lucidly maintained his analysis until the end of his days. In these last years, the content of his speeches, his interaction with questioners, and his capacity to discuss major issues with world leaders reveal a still active mind. Donald Soper, in describing him at this time, said:

> There was a sense of vitality. He was passionate about the causes he represented but very much the master of his own feelings and emotions.

Next, it is false to paint Lansbury as some kind of lone peace ranger who spouted a sentimental view that no sensible people would back. The famous Peace Ballot of 1934 revealed over ten million people wanting Britain to reduce armaments and a large majority in favour of non-military sanctions against aggressors. As Thomson observed:

> The idea that Fascist dictators would submit to non-military coercion, when they knew their opponents had no intention

of resisting might with might, was a favourable belief in the thirties.[17]

Far from being an odd, maverick figure, Lansbury expressed the views of thousands of citizens.

Nor is there truth in the accusations that Lansbury was blind to what was happening in Germany and Italy. On the contrary, he was one of those who tried to awaken Britain to the evils and in the early 1930s wrote of 'the complete suppression of all freedom of press, speech, or organisation, of deliberate and organised murders and floggings' in Germany.[18] Moreover, Lansbury continuously strove to protect refugees, particularly Jewish ones, from Fascist states. Co-operating with the Society of Friends Germany Emergency Committee and the Co-ordinating Committee for Refugees, he besought an often unwilling home secretary to give sanctuary to those who fled from Germany, Austria and Czechoslovakia. For those who were denied permission to stay in Britain, he tried to arrange visas to New Zealand or South America. Right up to the last weeks of his life, Lansbury was pleading with the government to allow a German Jew, Erich Stern, to stay in Britain.

So Lansbury was well aware of and publicly condemned the injustices committed by Germany and her allies. At the same time, and unlike many others in the Commons, he was prepared to admit that Britain and her allies had imposed an unjust economic settlement upon Germany in 1919. Therefore one of his major aims, in visiting foreign heads, was to pave the way for an economic conference which would facilitate peaceful relationships through fairer economic and trading arrangements. It was this intent which took him to Germany in 1937, where he straightaway drew attention to the 'tremendous system of espionage and control', saying that 'many people are spied upon and put away because of fake evidence'.[19] Nor was he likely to be taken in by Hitler, for already he had savagely attacked his 'frantic nationalist creed of egoism and hatred'.[20] After speaking with Hitler, he commented wryly that:

as I listened to him I imagined myself listening to speeches that I had heard in our House of Commons defending concentration camps in South Africa and the actions of the Black and Tans in Ireland.[21]

Certainly, Lansbury did come away believing that Hitler wanted to avoid war with Britain and France. He was not alone in that. Later, Chamberlain believed the same and took most of the Commons with him. Moreover, A.J.P. Taylor now writes, 'It is hard to believe that he [Hitler] wanted a full-scale war against Great Britain and France,' and he reasons that Hitler's strategy of war against minor powers later went wrong and led to the events which did culminate in world war.[22] One thing is certain: Hitler could not be relied upon and his invasion of Austria only confirmed for Lansbury, as he said, that 'Hitler cannot be trusted'.[23]

Lansbury then was under no illusions about what was going on in Germany. Nor was he taken in by Hitler more than most of his contemporaries. His misjudgment was to think that he — as an individual emissary of a small, voluntary committee rather than as a representative of a country or political party — could sway the mind and actions of national leaders.

Lansbury's tour of European heads was simply part of his sincere belief that he had to do something, anything, to try to avoid war. Lansbury was not just a theoretical pacifist. He had seen war on the Western front. He had met the results of war in the disabled ex-soldiers begging in the streets and in the poverty-stricken widows in the East End. He could not bear the thought of a repeat of all that suffering. Further, his pacifism rested on a Christianity which he was always trying to apply to his actions. He declared:

> But Christians whose faith rests on the incarnation, who believe that the coming of Jesus as the Son of God sanctified all human life, cannot possibly believe it is God's will that men should fight and destroy each other.[24]

As a Christian, Lansbury felt he had to be a peacemaker. Donald Soper put it this way: 'He believed, as I do, that pacifism was more a matter of obedience than a matter of calculation.' Thus Lansbury's experience of war and his experience as a servant of Christ combined to compel him to take some action to avert human slaughter.

Michael Foot, who knew Lansbury well by this time, has pointed out that Lansbury knew well that his actions would not receive the support of his beloved Labour Party and that he knew he would be sneered at and misunderstood. Foot himself believed that Lansbury was mistaken in his mission. But, he added:

The reason why he did it was absolutely honourable. He was desperately anxious about the world going into war and he thought he would do something to help stop it. He wasn't worried about his reputation on that account.

Of course, the task was beyond Lansbury or any other individual. Nonetheless, the readiness of a man of his age to travel so many miles was a tribute to his commitment to peace, and the readiness of foreign heads to receive him was a tribute to his international standing as a man of peace. He failed, but no other person in the Western world tried harder to prevent a war which, as Lansbury rightly foresaw, would cost millions of precious human lives.

In February 1939, Lansbury paused for a family gathering to celebrate his birthday. Delighted by a cake with eighty candles, he was even more pleased to have all thirty-two grandchildren around him. Then, as war seemed just a matter of time, he continued his peace efforts. He cabled Hitler and Mussolini asking them to heed Roosevelt's plea for a peace conference. On 28 April, he wrote an impassioned article in the *Daily Sketch* saying:

> I write not as a censorious judge of others, but as one who has discovered through long years of experience that Jesus truly has the words of eternal life. We must learn the path to peace through him . . .

In July, he went to Belgium to encourage its leaders to initiate a European peace and economic conference.

All was in vain. Britain had made a treaty with Poland and, when Hitler invaded that country, Britain regretfully declared war on Germany on 3 September 1939. That same day, Lansbury was listened to with quiet respect in the Commons when he admitted:

> The cause that I and a handful of friends represent is this morning apparently going down to ruin . . . I hope that out of this terrible calamity will arise a spirit that will compel people to give up reliance on force.

Lansbury was now in very poor health as cancer took a grip on his body. Yet he refused to retire. When, in the Commons,

Winston Churchill sneered at conscientious objectors as those with 'easy, comfortable lives' who were unwilling to make sacrifices for others, Lansbury rose angrily to retort that he had dwelt all his days among people who had no comforts and who made enormous sacrifices yet who might still oppose war. Simultaneously, Lansbury was also urging caution on the PPU practice of picketing employment exchanges where men registered for the forces. The picketing provoked much hostility and Lansbury worried that the government might remove the rights of conscientious objectors and revert to the harsh practices used against their forerunners in the 1914–18 war.

In January 1940, several MPs nominated Lansbury for the Nobel Peace Prize. He was not unduly concerned, partly because honours meant little to him and partly because he knew he was soon to die. He continued to show his love for all his family and travelled to visit thirteen-year-old Terry who had undergone an operation for peritonitis. Terry recalled:

> Although himself in pain and deeply depressed by the war news, his only concern was for my recovery and putting on his most cheerful face he roared, 'Come on young Terry me lad, we can't have two of us swinging the lead.'[25]

By April, he felt too ill to attend the PPU annual conference. Abroad, German troops had marched into Denmark and Norway. Somehow he managed his usual smiles and retained his sense of humour. When a journalist knocked on his door for an interview, Lansbury pretended to be the butler. He tidied up his papers and then penned his final article, which appeared in *Tribune* on 26 April. In it, he declared that he remained 'an unashamed, solid-as-a-rock-of-granite pacifist'. His last written words were these:

> I hold fast to the truth that this world is big enough for all; that we are all brethren, children of one Father. It is not His fault that we misuse this world because the fault is in ourselves. I beg all my readers to join, not in creating a new British world, but a new world wherein will be practised the true way of life: 'Each for all and all for each.'

Soon after, Lansbury was admitted to the TUC Manor House Hospital. His last spoken words were ones of hope for the PPU and concern for daughter Annie, who was almost penniless. On 7 May 1940, he died in the arms of his son, William.

Lansbury's body lay at his beloved 39 Bow Road until carried the short distance to St Mary's Church. The rector conducted a service packed with leading politicians, foreign ambassadors and, what Lansbury would have liked best, the ordinary people of Bow and Poplar. At Ilford Crematorium, the congregation rose spontaneously to sing the Red Flag. A few days later, at a memorial service in Westminster Abbey, they sang his favourite:

> I will not cease from mental fight,
> Nor shall my sword sleep in my hand,
> Till we have built Jerusalem
> In England's green and pleasant land.

In his will, Lansbury stipulated that his ashes be scattered at sea, writing, 'I desire this because although I love England very dearly . . . I am a convinced internationalist.' He left little else. The house where he spent most of his life was soon afterwards destroyed by bombs. Attempts were made to preserve his memory as streets, gardens, a youth centre and a stained glass window in Kingsley Hall were named after him. The Lansbury Estate was built in the East End as the 'living architecture' exhibition for the 1951 Festival of Britain. More important, he left children and grandchildren who loved him. His devoted Annie was rehoused, after the war, in a new council estate in Ilford where she supported the tenants' association and the peace movement. In 1951, a year before she died, she joined the Communist Party, saying that the Labour Party had lost its socialist roots. Granddaughter Angela was evacuated to America where she subsequently achieved fame as a film and TV star. Most of the Lansburys remained socialists and, as late as 1974, grandson Terry was standing as a Labour parliamentary candidate.

So Lansbury left few material valuables but many human ones. He also left the memory and example of a life committed to beliefs and principles. Its impact was powerful and widespread.

References

1 Terry Lansbury, letter to the author.

2 Ibid.

3 Professor John Postgate, letter to the author.

4 G. Lansbury, *My Quest for Peace*, Michael Joseph Ltd., 1938, p. 34.

5 M. Ceadle, *Pacifism in Britain 1914–1945*, Clarendon Press, 1980, p. 36.

6 S. Morrison, *I Renounce War: the Story of the Peace Pledge Union*, Sheppard Press, 1962, chapter 1.

7 Private communication from Professor W. Fishman, letter to the author.

8 V. Brittain, *Testament of Experience*, Fontana Paperbacks, 1980, p. 164.

9 F. Brockway, *Bermondsey Story. The Life of Alfred Salter*, Allen and Unwin, 1949, pp. 198–99.

10 B. Pimlott, *Hugh Dalton*, Cape, 1985, p. 225.

11 Lansbury, *Quest for Peace*, p. 141.

12 Ibid., p. 130.

13 Ibid., p. 286.

14 E. Shinwell, *I've Lived Through It All*, Gollancz Ltd., 1973, p. 131.

15 R. Postgate, *The Life of George Lansbury*, Longmans, Green & Co., 1951, p. 308.

16 A.J.P. Taylor, *English History 1914–1945*, Penguin Books, reprinted 1987, p. 553.

17 D. Thomson, *England in the Twentieth Century*, Jonathan Cape, 1964, p. 133.

18 G. Lansbury, *My England*, Selwyn and Blount Ltd., 1934, p. 194.

19 Lansbury, *Quest for Peace*, p. 133.

20 Lansbury, *My England*, p. 193.

21 Lansbury, *Quest for Peace*, p. 138.

22 Taylor, *English History*, p. 580.

23 Lansbury, *Quest for Peace*, p. 135.

24 Lansbury, *My England*, p. 42.

25 Terry Lansbury, letter to the author.

10
LANSBURY

Lansbury's political career, in local and central government, covered over fifty years. Yet, aside from the publications of relatives, no book has been written about him. Even the biography by his son-in-law contains no assessment of his contribution, for Postgate considered that he wrote too soon after his death. This chapter is an attempt to evaluate Lansbury's long life.

Socialist

Lansbury was not always a socialist. From his youth, human suffering disturbed him deeply. He felt distress at the sight of families crowded eight to a room, at unemployed men fighting each other for jobs, at women torn from their children upon entering the workhouse. He felt anger at the contrast between the large houses and numerous servants of the rich employers in Greenwich and the hovels in the East End. He often wrote about the sterling qualities of poor people, their solidarity and neighbourliness, yet he never romanticized about poverty. He knew that it led to insecurity, ill-health and shortened life expectancy. In his twenties, Lansbury began to ask why such poverty and inequality existed. He concluded that the answer was the system of capitalism with its emphasis on material greed and on divisions between the holders of wealth and workers. Moreover, he perceived that even within a so-called democratic country, capitalism meant that small elites dominated parliamentary, industrial and voluntary institutions to the exclusion of working-class people. From this analysis, Lansbury moved on to the solution, namely socialism, which he saw as a system based on co-operation, which distributed goods according to need, which regarded all people as of equal worth and which spread power throughout society. The Rev. William Lax, himself a prominent Poplar Liberal, described Lansbury's change from Liberal to socialist as follows:

> I first met him in the early days when Socialism was a voice crying in the wilderness. He was then an ardent Liberal in politics. Gradually, Liberalism became suspect. It was too slow and lukewarm for his eager spirit. With his passionate love for the poor, and his overwhelming enthusiasm for their betterment, there could be no other course than out-and-out Socialism for him, and he jumped in at the deep end. He has never retracted, never regretted, never turned back.

Socialism does not describe a single entity. Lansbury was a democratic socialist. As a young man, Lansbury parted company with those who argued that socialism could be achieved only by force. Later, he rejoiced in the Russian revolution and the overthrow of the oppressive Tsarist system but he never supported Communism with its imposition of a one-party state. He declared that:

> there must be no ambiguity about our intentions and no hesitancy in our determination to use all constitutional means to attain our ends. Fascists and Communists are united in saying that Parliament which has completed many political revolutions cannot accomplish a social and economic one. It is our proud privilege to prove they are wrong.[2]

Lansbury held to democracy because the ballot box offered a peaceful rather than a violent means to change. But there was more to it than that. He wrote:

> My objective in all my propaganda is to make such people realise that it is their individual task to reform or revolutionise society and that democratic action is impossible without them.[3]

In other words, Lansbury believed that socialism could only be established to endure if it truly rested on the consent of the people and that that consent could be expressed only within a democratic process.

Not least, Lansbury had faith that socialism really would be achieved by democratic means. He had participated in a movement by which socialists had been elected to a majority on the Board of Guardians. Similarly, he had witnessed the Labour Party take control of the Poplar Borough Council. He had watched the Labour Party gradually increase its numbers in the Commons and he foresaw the day when it would possess an overall majority there. Socialism could and would be won by democratic means.

As a democratic socialist, Lansbury therefore strove to extend democracy. He campaigned for votes for all women and all men. In addition, he wanted social agencies to be democratically controlled. Thus he was opposed to the setting up of semi-autonomous bodies, such as the UAB, which were fully financed by government but not directly responsible to the House of Commons. Further, he was aware of the dangers of sham democracy, the creation of elected institutions to which only the powerful and the privileged were in a position to be elected. Accordingly, he saw the limitations of voluntary bodies whose elected committees and top officials almost always excluded people from working-class backgrounds. Again, although in favour of public corporations to run major industries, he was against the model in which board members were appointed by ministers and civil servants. He predicted that such an approach would continue the domination of the establishment in running industry. He wanted industrial matters 'decided by those chosen by the workers themselves'.[4] Lansbury argued for a democracy that applied to all institutions and to all people.

Lansbury was also an ethical socialist. As Geoffrey Foote shows, the early founders of the Labour Party included those who looked for a society based on different ethical principles from those which underpinned capitalism.[5] Lansbury stood with them. His concern was not limited to winning elections and exercising power for its own sake. To him, socialism was about creating a new society based on a new footing. His writings and speeches are full of references to right and wrong, justice and injustice, love and hatred. Harold Laski, writing of him in 1931, stated:

> Other men may see farther or more clearly; no man sees more justly than George Lansbury. I should not necessarily feel that I was wrong if I differed with him on intellectual grounds. I should certainly feel unhappy if I differed from him on ethical principle. For in that realm he has a definite genius for being in the right.[6]

More recently, the present Lord Tonypandy, George Thomas, said:

> There was nothing Marxist about him. For him it was a moral movemeni, about social justice. It was not just a struggle for power, it was a struggle for values — and that put him head and shoulders above men like Herbert Morrison and Ernie Bevin.

With the death of Keir Hardie, Lansbury more than any other Labour politician preached socialism from an ethical base. Norman Dennis and A.H. Halsey, in their study *English Ethical Socialism*, examine a number of important ethical socialists and from their writings identify six common features. They state: 'First, second and third are positive commitments to fraternity, liberty and equality'; the fourth is a rejection of the view that society's future is 'ineluctable and will be the result of social laws working themselves out with an iron necessity towards an inevitable goal', the fifth is a recognition that past history has shaped present institutions and morality, the sixth is 'a shared belief in the power of moral character to perfect a person and ennoble a nation'.[7]

Lansbury possessed the same commitments. He constantly argued that individual liberty and collective fraternity could only flourish in a society where rights, opportunities and resources were distributed equally. He drew upon an historical analysis to understand the injustices of the present and did so in order to stimulate change for he dismissed any ideas of inevitability. He certainly believed in the power of moral character although he would have quibbled at the notion of the attainability of perfection in this present life.

Lansbury, then, fits into the kind of ethical socialism described by Dennis and Halsey. Yet he differed from the notable characters cited by them as examples of modern ethical socialists. People such as Hobhouse, Orwell, Tawney and Marshall were essentially academics and authors who lectured to and wrote for an intellectual and middle-class audience. By contrast, Lansbury always lived amongst and preached to working-class people. He stands as the socialist who took ethical socialism to the back streets, to the factory workers, to dockers, to the unemployed and to disenfranchised women. More, he showed that they too could appreciate and respond to calls for a socialism based on love of one's neighbour, on justice, on principle.

Being an ethical socialist did not mean Lansbury had his head in the clouds. He was also a practical socialist. He was prepared to work through the imperfect machinery of the Poor Law. He pointed out that government and voluntary work schemes were mere palliatives, not cures for unemployment. Yet he supported them, for he wrote in a foreword to a booklet on work schemes that:

> none of us with eyes to see and heart and brain to understand
> dare stand idly by and watch the moral and mental distress
> which afflicts so many of our people, without making some
> effort to stem the tide of demoralisation.'[8]

More, he knew that ethics had to be translated into precise aims and policies for a future Labour government. On returning from his illness in 1934, he wrote a stirring article in the *Herald* of 5 June stating that Labour's three immediate aims would be the abolition of unemployment, the provision of decent homes and the organization of a 'health-for-all' service. He followed this with *My England*, in which he outlined the steps by which Labour would build a socialist society. The major industries, land and banks would come under public ownership and be used co-operatively for the good of all rather than for the profit, power and status of the few. Indeed, Lansbury here defined socialism 'as a policy which organises industry for use and not for profit — which in turn means for the use of all as a matter of right, not of charity'.[9] With land and industry developed for all, Lansbury foresaw a growth in production, the creation of more jobs and increased consumption which, in turn, would reduce unemployment. As for wages he said that:

> these will be fixed nationally by an authority made up of
> representatives of all industries including every section, and
> will be as far as is humanly possible equal. I want a classless
> England, and wish for equal pay and conditions.[10]

Industrial re-organization and wage equalization would lead, Lansbury argued, to the death of the twin terrors of unemployment and poverty. But national social services would be required for other purposes. He placed much importance on 'the provision of nurseries and nursery schools for young children . . . because we shall not be so silly as to try and prevent women working'[11] From nursery schools, children would proceed to a much improved school system in which the talents of all children would be encouraged and developed. As to health, Lansbury perceived that improved work environments, housing and diet would do much to prevent illness. More specialized treatment would come through a national medical service supplied on the basis of need, not ability to pay. Moreover, sick pay and pensions would be sufficient for their recipients to maintain adequate standards of living.

Lansbury added much more detail in his comprehensive blueprint for a socialist nation. To be sure, he left a number of questions unanswered. What would be the role of trade unions in wage negotiations? He did not explain where small private entrepreneurs — such as shopkeepers — would fit in, for he appeared to accept their continued existence. None the less, Lansbury did produce many concrete proposals which showed that he was far more than a 'pie in the sky' socialist. He wrote:

> Readers will understand that I am not what is styled an
> intellectual or literary person, but what I write, even if it is
> not written with literary elegance, is, I hope, clear and direct.[12]

Certainly, Lansbury could not claim to be an academic. But his plans for a future socialist government were both clear and practical.

Christian

Clearly, Lansbury was a socialist. Just as clearly he was a Christian, and in some ways a very orthodox one. A member of the Church of England, he believed in a personal God whose Holy Spirit dwelt within believers. He believed in prayer, saying, 'I know that for me prayer is an inspiration and that it leads to work and renewed effort.'[13] He believed in Christ as the Son of God and based his life on the teaching 'which our Saviour taught two thousand years ago.'[14] Lansbury's spiritual confidant in his last years was the Rev. Father Andrew who often administered communion to him. In a letter, written after Lansbury's death and now lodged in the Lansbury Collection, Father Andrew wrote that Lansbury believed:

> that Christ always was God, One with the eternal Father: that for

171

our sakes He became Man . . . and that through the Holy Spirit mediates the benefits of His Passion and the power of His life to believing disciples.

In other ways, Lansbury was unorthodox and certainly different from the more numerous Nonconformist socialists who attended strict chapels. He expressed tolerance towards all kinds of Christians and to members of other faiths. In 1914, at the invitation of Annie Besant, he joined the Theosophical Society which tried to unite all faiths. In his grief-stricken days following the death of Bessie he even showed an interest in Spiritualism. Postgate said that he disliked Roman Catholicism 'because it interposed a priest between man and his conscience'.[15] Lansbury may not have agreed with that particular role for a priest but he never showed any hostility towards Catholics. On the contrary, he had great admiration for Catholic MPs such as John Wheatley, and he spoke well of the way in which many Irish priests identified with the poor. In his youthful days, he spoke in a debate in favour of tolerating the papacy. Lansbury held strong convictions but he did not want to impose them on others and advocated freedom of expression for all other religions and for atheism. Similarly, he never tried to impose his teetotalism, non-gambling or church-going on others. Of the latter, he wrote, 'I never have seen anything wrong in going to a morning service on Sunday and afterwards taking a day's outing in the country.'[16]

Whether orthodox or unorthodox, Lansbury made no secret of his Christianity. His books and articles continually refer to his faith. What he said and did as a Christian had much effect on others. For instance, an anonymous contributor to the April 1933 issue of an East End Catholic church magazine wrote:

We younger men will never be able to say what we owe to George Lansbury from the example he has set us all, of a consistent self-sacrificing life, of a constant and fearless witness to Jesus Christ.

In a letter, now in the Lansbury Collection, a Quaker, Fred Hellowell, records that he was struck by Lansbury's prayer at a meeting:

It was not what he said, it was the earnestness of the man, it was the deep sincerity and humility of one who knew Christ, and of one who wanted his brothers and sisters to know Jesus as he knew him.

The Methodist George Thomas said:

He didn't call himself a born again Christian but he was and he witnessed to his Christian faith in his politics.

Perhaps most telling, the non-believer, Harold Laski, wrote:

Profoundly religious, George Lansbury makes the freethinker respect the inspiration of an inner faith as not half a dozen Englishmen in the last fifty years.[17]

Lansbury's Christianity received public attention partly because he was also a socialist. He was unusual in being an Anglican socialist in an era in which the Church of England remained closely identified with the establishment. Within some Anglican circles, private property and the existing class system were still regarded as ordained by God and hence Lansbury's brand of socialism was regarded as un-Christian. Lansbury, however, argued the opposite. His socialism and Christianity were closely connected in three particular ways.

First, Lansbury drew the majority of his socialist principles and practices directly from his understanding of Christianity. Foremost stood his belief in equality. All people, whatever their sex or race, were created by and valued by God. The same God had made a world full of abundance and, as he also decreed that people should love one another, it was an abundance to be shared. This love reflected the fact that all had a common Father and were thus related in terms of brotherhood and sisterhood. True, people were born with the freedom to choose evil but also the capacity to choose good. The ties of brotherhood should be used to encourage the latter so that people were brought together in systems of co-operation not conflict, of peace not war. Not least, Lansbury perceived that the early Christians did put these godly principles into earthly practice. He wrote:

The disciples held all things in common and they refused . . . to carry arms or rely on force . . . Their message, not changed in essence in the twenty centuries since the crucifixion, but only applied with commonsense to modern conditions, is the message in which I firmly believe as a Socialist.[18]

Second, as is implied in the above quotation, Lansbury regarded socialism as the political system whereby such principles were most likely to be put into practice. Socialism entailed the replacement of capitalism by that of corporate ownership. It therefore lent itself to a more equal distribution of goods and power which was in keeping with the Christian basis of equality. Socialism was about co-operation and fraternity which were closely allied to Christian love and brotherhood. Lansbury had no doubt that in striving for a socialist society he was simultaneously seeking a Christian one and vice versa. Thus:

> in a Christian society no person would have two homes until every person was able to secure one; no person would be allowed luxurious food until everybody was able to afford the food necessary for sustaining a decent standard of life.[19]

Lansbury was careful to point out that socialism could be built on the value systems of people who were not Christians. Indeed, his own socialist convictions remained strong during the period when he felt alienated from the church. He acknowledged that not all Christians became socialists. However, he reckoned that they *ought* to do so. He argued that the Old Testament condemned usury, which was the basis of the capitalist system, while the New Testament revealed the principle and practice of loving one's neighbour which was inconsistent with the continuation of class divisions and of poverty in the midst of affluence. He declared:

> We cannot show our reverence and love of God through crushing our enemy in the dust or forcing our business competitor into bankruptcy.[20]

He continued that Christians ought to be socialists:

> Socialism, which means love, co-operation, and brotherhood in every department of human affairs, is the only outward expression of a Christian faith.[21]

Indeed, after his reflections in hospital, he stated that his faith in socialism:

> is always unquestionable, simply because it is founded on the solid rock of conviction that it is the will of God that all His children shall enjoy the fullness of life which this world of abundance can give to all.[22]

Lansbury thus proclaimed the closest of connections between Christianity and socialism. In so doing he was of help to many who were striving to reconcile the two. Typical was Jim Simmons, later an MP, but writing of his younger days in pre-1914 Birmingham. He wrote:

> Beatrice and I, two young Christians who felt the poverty we met in the homes of our Sunday-school scholars should be engaging the attention of the church. We went to hear George Lansbury; his message was just what we had been waiting for; according to him not only were Christianity and Socialism not incompatible but Capitalism and Christianity were.[23]

Third, he claimed that Christianity could motivate and empower people to live as socialists. He wanted legislation to redistribute wealth, to equalize incomes, to enable working-class men and women to take on positions of responsibility. Yet, in a democracy, such profound changes would depend on the will of individuals. As he said, 'I cannot believe in any change being real unless it starts from individual men and women.'[24] In other words, a socialist society could not be created without socialists. But often men and women, even if convinced in their minds of the socialist case, did not strive for and live for socialism. They needed an enabling power and Lansbury stated:

> I have come to believe that the motive power which should and which *will* if men allow it, work our social salvation, is the power which comes from a belief in Christ and his message to man.[25]

This view of the motivating power of Christianity entails some difficulties. As Lansbury acknowledged, some non-Christians were motivated to be fine socialists. Lansbury's reply, not always very clear, was that they were still empowered by a more general God-given love. Other people, though, not least himself, could only live the socialist life as they were transformed by the direct intervention of God himself. Of one thing he was sure: if people turned to God, if they took seriously his commands, if they followed the example of Christ, then they would strive to bring about a socialist society.

In these three ways Lansbury's Christianity influenced, even-shaped, his socialism. In addition, as a prominent socialist, he influenced the church. Since the nineteenth century, there had existed a small but articulate group within Anglican circles called Christian Socialists. Their founding father is usually considered to be the Rev. F.D. Maurice, with Thomas Hughes and Charles Kingsley as other important supporters. Interestingly, Lansbury never identified with and rarely referred to them. The probable reason is that he would not have regarded them as socialists. Edward Norman, in his study of these Victorian Christian Socialists, shows that they were opposed to most collective action by the state with Maurice declaring, 'Property is holy, distinction of ranks is holy.'[26] To them, socialism meant the church becoming more aware of social issues and being prepared to advise members how to behave in the secular world.

As shown in chapter two, Lansbury did identify with the Church Socialist League, became its president in 1912, and spoke at many of its meetings. The League was committed to Lansbury's kind of socialism and made its presence felt at several church congresses. Consisting mainly of high churchmen, it suffered a blow in 1918 when Conrad Noel, a prominent theologian, broke away to form the Catholic Crusade. However, Richard Tawney — whose ethical socialism was very similar to that of Lansbury — became a member and helped the League formulate its views on just how the church could act in socialist ways.[27] The League only survived a few more years but, in 1960, some twenty years after Lansbury's death, had a successor in the Christian Socialist Movement which, under the chair of Donald Soper, called for Christians of all denominations to work for the common ownership of major resources and for a classless society.

Lansbury also wrote frequently about socialism in Christian papers, particularly the *Church Times*. Postgate recorded that 'it was said, and may have been true, that in the thirties George Lansbury's voice was more influential in the Church than the average bishop's'.[28] He tried to persuade the church to speak out against social problems, particularly unemployment and poverty. He wanted church members to understand that a socialist society was in keeping with a Christian society. He faced trememdous opposition, for the Church of England remained overwhelmingly conservative in attitude and Conservative in politics. Yet Lansbury did show the church that a responsible cabinet minister could be both Christian and socialist. In so doing, he probably made the prospect of a future Labour government more acceptable to many church members.

Christianity and socialism dominated Lansbury's very being. In the former, he found the principles and power of living. In the latter, he found the system through which they could be expressed. Together he believed they would lead to a society where poverty and unemployment would be no more, where conditions of equality would facilitate fraternity, and where the practice of all would be characterized by love. So strong were his beliefs that they compelled him into three directions which sum up his main contributions to the Labour movement and to a better society.

Believing that the socialist faith had to be spread, that people needed to become socialists before there could be socialism, that Christians needed to be persuaded that socialism was the earthly expression of their religion, that working people needed to be called into the Labour Party and that existing socialists needed to be encouraged, Lansbury became one of socialism's great prophets.

Believing that socialism was more important than his own career or status, Lansbury was willing to participate in any activity for the cause. His physical strength, his firm convictions and his inner serenity enabled him to be a participant in an astonishing number of roles, any one of which would have fully tested most people.

Believing that faith had to be applied to personal living, Lansbury became a socialist practitioner. As a Christian, he was captivated by the Christ who applied the principle of love to himself to the extent that he came to earth as an ordinary carpenter and submitted to a cruel death for the sake of others. Of all the Christian saints Lansbury was most impressed by Francis of Assisi, who applied Christ's injunctions to himself by renouncing material luxuries and by living among and serving the poorest people. In like manner, Lansbury attempted to show that a socialism derived from Christianity was more than a political system, it was a way of living.

Prophet

Lansbury's involvement with Labour politics stretched from 1892 to 1940. During that period, he held cabinet office for a mere two years yet for all forty-eight years he was continuously preaching socialism, travelling thousands of miles to speak in halls, in factories, in the open air. He thus described himself as a 'socialist propagandist' with the aim of 'winning men and women to socialism'.[29] Harold Laski said:

> Mr Lansbury's job has been to act as the evangelist of the movement. Day in, day out, he has preached its gospel. He has lit a flame in thousands of hearts.[30]

Lansbury lived in a time when the Labour Party was established as the party of many working people and he played a major part in that establishment.

Lansbury also wrote hundreds of articles and some popular books about socialism. But, in an age without television, the spoken word at public meetings was still a major means of communication and it was here that Lansbury excelled. His effectiveness as a speaker was revealed in the first two decades of the century when he was one of the very few politicians able to fill the Royal Albert Hall. Invitations to address meetings regularly dropped through his letter box and he responded to as many as possible. Many newspaper reports spoke enthusiastically of his powerful impact. In later years, his presence was in demand at every by-election contested by Labour and in many constituencies in general elections. As Jim Simmons in Birmingham put it 'no election campaign would have been fully effective unless G.L. had spoken at several meetings'.[31] And, in the Commons, Michael Foot commented, 'He was a wonderful speaker . . . He was a great emotional speaker but he was also an extremely able arguer and debater. He had a great command of words.'

What made Lansbury such an outstanding speaker? He offered no erudite learning. His voice — rasping, loud and cockney — could not be compared with the beauty and lilt of MacDonald or Lloyd George. In his younger days, his blond hair and bright blue eyes gave him an attractive presence but the hair was to thin and fade. The explanation is found in the following quotations from people who heard him. An unnamed reporter, in the *Pioneer* paper of December 1918, wrote that:

> he speaks straight out of the fulness of his heart, and therefore his words fly straight to all hearts that are not resolutely shut against them by prejudice . . . he speaks of the elementary facts of common human knowledge, and of the life and death of ordinary men and women . . . of the ways and means of fighting onwards out of the valley of despair into the sunshine.

Twenty years later, Harold Laski stated:

> The answer, I think, is that he has a peculiar genius. He represents the urgency to do the right thing, the sense that to act by the light of one's conscience matters as nothing else matters, that no effort can possibly be wasted if the end is worth while.[32]

In the 1930s, the Rev. Allan Harling frequently chaired political meetings addressed by Lansbury. He remembered:

> He was a very simple straightforward type of speaker . . . No cheap or clever witticisms to score a point or jibe on an opponent. Just an honest-to-God fellow with a few notes on a couple of dog-eared postcards. It was the shining sincerity of the man which captured the audience. What he *was* was more important than even what he said.[33]

And Clem Attlee, looking back at Lansbury's life in *The Times* of 20 February 1959, wrote:

> During the last years of the nineteenth and the first decade of the twentieth century . . . he became known as one of the most forcible speakers on Socialist platforms . . . Lansbury's magnificent physique enabled him to undertake a tremendous programme while his passionate sincerity had a great effect.

Lansbury thus spoke about socialism in words which ordinary people could comprehend, with a passion that compelled their attention, with an ethic which touched their emotions, and with a sincerity that convinced them of the truth of his message. They flocked to hear him and he won the ears and hearts of thousands. In the history of socialism, Lansbury must rank with Keir Hardie as the great oral communicator of the Labour Party's message. But he outlived Hardie by over twenty years and in the 1920s and 1930s he became the foremost Labour speaker.

Lansbury's speeches made a powerful impression on many individuals. For instance, Naomi Mitchison often heard him in the 1930s and recorded, 'Once I watched him carefully while he made one of those marvellously moving speeches; he would glance at his watch and then shift key, carrying us with him.'[34] She was profoundly affected by his words.

But Lansbury influenced individuals through more than his addresses. He gave his personal attention to Labour supporters. He spent time with Jim Simmons and encouraged him to accept the cause of women's rights as a part of socialism. After his visit to the meeting organized by George Thomas, he wrote him a hand-written, four-page letter about the need for idealism in socialism and encouraged the young Thomas to play his part in the Labour movement. Thus Lansbury promoted the development of many notable socialists. The renowned intellectual, Harold Laski, wrote of Lansbury — who received little formal schooling — the following tribute:

> I know of no education in citizenship greater than association with him on some cause. Nothing you do seems unimportant; you always find yourself able to do more than you expected to attempt . . . I am only one of many who owe their first real chance to George Lansbury; and when he enlisted me in his army, he made me feel that I had found, not an employer, but a friend.[35]

In the Lansbury Collection are letters from others who also called him 'a friend'. Unlike Laski, they were ordinary, now unknown socialists. Yet Lansbury regarded them all as important and took time to encourage both their personal and political growth.

Lansbury's rapport with large audiences allied with his genuine concern for individuals gave rise to what is the most common and remarkable comment made about him — that he was loved. In his history of socialism in London, Armstrong observes that 'perhaps the most deeply loved of all the leaders of the London working people' was Lansbury.[36] At the *Herald*, Geoffrey Goodman recalled that the chief librarian 'spoke of him with love and awe.'[37] The same emotion was engendered nationally when he became established as an MP. George Thomas said, 'To the party and in the country, even when he was no longer leader, he was loved, he really was loved.' And Fred Hellowell, who knew Lansbury in his last years with the Peace Pledge Union, stated in a letter now in the Lansbury Collection:

> One just could not help loving George Lansbury because there was nothing that was not love in his heart. He radiated something that overcame our pettiness and our sense of rank and position.

Of course, not everyone loved George Lansbury. John Postgate recalled that at school he heard the well-to-do parents of one pupil declaring that GL should be shot.[38] Within the Labour Party, there is little doubt that MacDonald disliked him while Bevin and Dalton poured scorn on his emotions and his conscience. Some left-wing socialists sneered at his Christianity. Some churchmen were enraged at what they regarded as his extremist political views. At some meetings he had abuse and missiles hurled at him. Yet for all the strong negative feelings which he aroused, it can hardly be disputed that he won and held the affection of a substantial number of the population. A.J.P. Taylor states that Lansbury was 'the most loveable figure in modern politics'.[39] This is noteworthy praise from a distinguished historian but probably Lansbury would have appreciated more the chants of children whenever he appeared at schools or playgrounds: 'Good old George.'

The Labour Party produced better organizers, more eloquent speakers, more intellectual figures than George Lansbury. Yet few others matched his passionate commitment, his capacity for expressing it in everyday language, and his genuine interest in individuals. By the 1930s, his name was synonymous with the Labour Party. If people wanted to know what a socialist was like then they looked to him. He had been present when the Labour Party first established itself in local and central politics. He had been loyal when others deserted. He possessed faith in the future establishment of socialism and he was regarded as its embodiment. Consequently, Lansbury was more than a propagandist, more than a socialist evangelist, more than a friend to individuals. He deserves the title prophet — one who was recognized as the representative and proclaimer of a movement and who was loved for so doing. Lansbury was truly a socialist prophet.

Participant

Lansbury's success as a communicator of socialism is sufficient to establish him as one of the great figures of the Labour movement in Britain. Yet, amazingly, he filled a large number of other positions. He was a socialist participant.

He was an energetic organizer. In his last years, Lansbury was sometimes dismissed as a sentimentalist, full of pious thoughts but lacking in realism and practicality. Nothing could be further from the truth. Lansbury cut his political teeth as a Liberal agent. So obvious was his skill at organizing at constituency level that the Liberals offered both financial inducements and a future seat in the Commons if he would work full-time for them. He declined and took on the unpaid and even more arduous job of organizing for the Social Democratic Federation where H.M. Hyndman conceded that he 'was on the whole the best organiser the Social Democratic Federation ever had.'[40] Later, Lansbury showed entrepreneurial abilities when he built up the wood mill business. While doing this, he was also running many large-scale demonstrations and campaigns, particularly in regard to unemployment and women's suffrage.

He was a successful journalist and editor. Despite his lack of schooling, Lansbury developed his own writing skills to the extent of writing numerous articles, many pamphlets and some books. Like Keir Hardie, he could have earned his living as a journalist. He then went beyond writing to participate in the founding of the *Daily Herald*. In turn, Lansbury served as its editor, manager and fund raiser and had the satisfaction of seeing it grow into the first mass-circulation Labour daily paper in Britain.

He did sterling service as a Poor Law Guardian. Lansbury was one of the first working-class members of the Poor Law Boards of Guardians. In Poplar, he and his colleagues gradually took control of the Board and then purged the system of corrupt officials before introducing a whole series of humane reforms. He then took the lead in policy developments to create training and work for unemployed men within the auspices of the Poor Law. His skill as an administrator and policy maker made him a national authority on the Poor Law, yet Lansbury always campaigned for its abolition and must have derived satisfaction from the gradual extension of local authority welfare services which paved the way for the end of the workhouse.

As a councillor, he served his community. While still a Guardian, Lansbury won election to Poplar Borough Council and became its first socialist mayor. He remained a councillor for the rest of his life and so served during a period of great expansion of municipal services. Moreover, he was prominent in the council's refusal to pay certain precepts, which in its struggle with central authority led to the word 'Poplarism' becoming part of the political vocabulary.

Lansbury's tenure as a cabinet minister lasted for a mere two years. Yet he was one of the few Labour successes in government and won the support of the civil service and the praise of much of the press for the drive and initiative he displayed as first commissioner for works.

Attention has already been drawn to Lansbury's contribution as leader of the Labour Party. The last word can be left with the one who succeeded him. Writing in *The Times* of 20 February 1959, Clem Attlee stated:

> He inspired and led for four years a little party of 45, many of whom were past doing much work, and made it into an effective opposition . . . Lansbury was successful in inspiring and leading this little band, thus, as Mr Baldwin said at the time, saving Parliamentary Government. A Labour member once said to a Conservative whip: 'I think G.L. is the best man I have known.' To which the Whip replied: 'Best, is that all? He's the ablest leader of the opposition I have ever seen.'

Many noteworthy socialists have contributed to the Labour movement in one particular sphere, in trade unions, in local government, in publications, in the Commons. Very few have been so successful in so many varied parts as George Lansbury. Moreover, for much of the time, he was carrying out these roles simultaneously. Yet Lansbury was not a seeker after power or status. He never cultivated contacts with the establishment or plotted with political allies to obtain posts either inside or outside of parliament. However, when jobs were offered to him — be it ward secretary or leader of the party — he was usually prepared to accept so that he could play his part in promoting socialism.

Practitioner

Lansbury's life was devoted to socialism — a socialism drawn from his Christianity. Yet, to him, socialism was not just about politics, not just about winning elections, not just about the future replacement of capitalism by a system of co-operation, it was also about a life to be lived in the present. Of all the admirable features about the man, the most impressive is that he was a practitioner of socialism. It may be that he was blessed with a cheerful temperament which helped him to be generous and loving. Yet there was also a deliberate application of the principles of socialism to his everyday relationships. Three aspects of his practitioner role deserve particular note: his integrity, his egalitarianism, and his fraternity.

During the early decades of the twentieth century, political standards came under fire. In 1912–13, the Marconi scandal led to allegations that some cabinet ministers had used their inside government information to make gains on the stock exchange. In 1922, Lloyd George's 'sale of honours' in return for contributions to party funds became an open secret. In 1931, many Labour supporters considered that MacDonald and his few followers had 'sold out' on their socialist principles in order to gain power and position. Lansbury was above all this. Even as a Poor Law Guardian, he declined to drink, feast or use the institution's billiard table at public expense. Later, he refused to use his standing as a well-known public figure to make money for himself. He would never accept fees for addressing socialist meetings. When, in 1934, the BBC sent him a cheque for a political broadcast he returned it. Later, he would not avail himself of his probable entitlement, as a former cabinet minister, to a pension.

One result of Lansbury's stand on principle was that he was sometimes in financial straits. In 1893, he wrote to the Sewells, declining an invitation to visit them, on the grounds that Bessie and he could not afford it. There followed the period of financial comfort when George ran the saw mill and timber business. But once he relinquished the firm, he was back to journalism — for he had no qualms about accepting fees from publishers who could afford it — and sometimes the salary of an MP. However, even the latter was low compared with the pay of today's MPs, for most were then expected to possess some other form of income. Of course, Lansbury was never in the poverty-stricken position of the unemployed. Yet he did accept many extra obligations towards his brothers and sisters, his children, his grandchildren, nephews and nieces. He also gave to neighbours in need, to charities, and to the branch of the local Labour Party. So, when Bessie died, their account in their London Co-operative Share Passbook amounted to £6-6-9d. When George died, he left very little.

Lansbury's behaviour contrasts sharply with that of some present-day Labour MPs who take on consultancies with outside firms to add to their now generous salaries. It contrasts with those who use their political standing and contacts as springboards into lucrative posts in the television or newspaper industries. No doubt, they would consider Lansbury a fool. So why did he refuse to enrich himself? One reason was that his commitment to socialism was more important than filling his wallet. Another was that he believed socialists had to demonstrate that they were above being bought out. The last was that he saw no reason why he should avail himself of financial privileges which were not available to the masses of people who voted for him. He wrote of himself and them:

> None of us will get rich: when I die I shall leave no property, no money, but we shall be able to say that together with thousands of other men and women we have striven to lift up the poor and oppressed and to bring help to those who are in need.[41]

Lansbury understood that to have enriched himself would have put a social and material gulf between himself and his comrades who were striving for socialism. His upright honesty and consistency which resulted deservedly won for him a national reputation as a man of integrity.

Lansbury believed passionately in the socialist aim of equality. The difficulty was how to practise it within an unequal society. He had little time for those — usually very affluent — socialists who treated equality just as a hope for the very distant future while they enjoyed the fruits of inequality in the present. He had respect for the ability of Sir Stafford Cripps but was uneasy about his weekend house parties for socialists in his country mansion, Filkins. Lansbury perceived that the practices of such socialists actually maintained inequality. He therefore tried to be egalitarian in two main ways. For a start, he insisted on distancing himself from the trappings of privilege. He never tried to ingratiate himself into the company of upper-class society, of the power holders in the mass media, the banks and industry. His son Edgar wrote that he:

> never attends the many impressive banquets given on great
> occasions by the Speaker, the Lord Mayor and other public
> functionaries . . . He has never been to a Royal Levee and in
> this, as a cabinet minister, has broken an unwritten law . . . in
> his view such affairs are a waste of time and money.[42]

He refused to wear robes when mayor of Poplar and, on becoming a cabinet minister, he provoked MacDonald's fury by refusing to wear knee-breeches when taking the oath. He looked upon such dress as symbolic of the very class differences he was out to abolish.

Next, Lansbury remained as close as he could to the working-class population of the East End. His house had more rooms — although it often had ten or more occupants — than the two-roomed dwellings of the poorest residents of Bow and Poplar. But it was located in the midst of his constituency and he refused to move from 39 Bow Road to the more respectable and healthier environments of rural Essex to the east, or royal Greenwich to the south. He once said to Father Groser:

> John, I would sooner be here in the Bow Rd where the
> unemployed can put a brick through my window when they
> disagree with my activities, than be in some other place far away
> where they can only write a letter.[43]

And come they did. Rarely to throw a brick, frequently to seek his ear. In 1929, Lansbury wrote in the *Evening Standard* of 14 September:

> My house in Bow has always been an open house. People come
> to see me at breakfast; they come at supper; and on Sundays
> they never stop coming in. Some of them come to talk, some for
> advice about money, rent or old-age pensions.

These words were penned while Lansbury was a cabinet minister. He would not allow even that position to cut him off from the everyday calls of the people of his neighbourhood.

One reason why ordinary folk felt free to knock on Lansbury's door was that his lifestyle remained not far removed from the many citizens to whom he chatted in the streets. He never spent much on clothes and was noted for his battered bowler, his reefer jacket and baggy trousers. He never possessed a car and travelled third class on the train. These actions were not some kind of inverted snobbery. Lansbury came from, belonged to and worked with and for the ordinary, working-class residents and, by his mode of life, he continued to be one of them. Unlike most of those residents, however, Lansbury could have obtained the means to move away from them both in distance and standard of living. He could have adopted what Frank Field calls the 'closed drawbridge mentality' in which those with access to affluence withdraw themselves from daily, living contact with poor people.[44] He declined because, as a socialist, he believed he should be closest to those for whom socialism could act as a liberating force. His decision did not go unnoticed. The Rev. Francis Gibbons, a Congregational minister brought up in Bow, wrote, 'How sad it was to see men like Ramsay MacDonald and J.H. Thomas gradually lose their fine qualities and compromise their ideals.'[45] Gibbons was not a man of strong political leanings but he went on to say how impressed he was by George Lansbury who kept his ideals and remained with his people. Years later, in 1970, George Thomas heard his colleagues in the Labour cabinet bemoaning the drop in salary they faced on leaving office. It made little difference to Thomas for, unlike them, he had not purchased a large house in London and had remained in his small home in South Wales. He attributed his action to the example of Lansbury and commented, 'I'm so pleased I did the same as G.L. He kept his values and his roots.' By putting the principle of equality into daily practice, Lansbury not only remained close to the people of Poplar and Bow; he also succeeded in persuading some others to follow his path.

Lastly, Lansbury practised fraternity. It seems that he found some difficulties in forming friendships with affluent socialists whose lifestyles and attitudes seemed out of tune with their principles. Edgar wrote, 'With one or two exceptions intimate friendships between him and middle and upper class people do not exist.'[46] In fact, the exceptions were more numerous than one or two. Joseph and Mary Fels were among George and Bessie's closest friends. For a while, Sylvia Pankhurst frequently visited their home. Lansbury worked closely with Annie Besant and the Lansbury Collection contains a number of letters from well-to-do people such as Mrs Coates Hansen and Murray MacDonald who valued

George and Bessie as friends. It should be added that George was warm and friendly towards anyone, not just socialists, who would work with and for the people of Poplar. For instance, Mrs Murray Guthrie was the wife of the Tory who defeated Lansbury in the election of 1900. After her husband died, she decided to stay in the East End and worked for many years, without publicity, at the Fern Street Settlement. Bessie and George enjoyed her company and he wrote that 'she makes life sweeter and kindlier for those to whom the struggle of life means worry and stress from one week's end to another'.[47]

But friendship is not quite the same as fraternity. By the latter, Lansbury meant the shared values, the sense of oneness, the feeling of fellowship based on a common purpose. This he experienced most deeply with the ordinary working-class men and women of the Labour movement and particularly those who dwelt in the east of London. They met on the pavement, in the shops, particularly the barber's shop, and in each others' homes. They shared innumerable political meetings, sometimes marching together to demonstrate on cold winter days, sometimes making their Labour plans in the relative comfort of the co-op halls where they were nourished by home-made sandwiches and cups of hot tea. Sometimes they would gather in the Lansbury home where, on one occasion, George — although in his seventies — lay on his back and kicked his legs in the air to prove that he was fit again.

It troubled George that he rather than his comrades received public notice. Consequently, his books contain lengthy lists of those whose names he wished to preserve. There was Jack Williams, who marched with him on many demonstrations; Docker Waite who campaigned for the unemployed on an empty stomach; Harry Orbell, another docker and fellow Christian, who constantly agitated for the poor; Charlie Sumner, a stoker and hard drinker, Mrs Savoy, a humble brushmaker who did good by sharing her life with others. In the preface of *My Life*, Lansbury mentions over sixty such comrades. They were the men and women who established trade unions and the Labour Party, who campaigned for votes for all, who served as Guardians and councillors, who went to prison with him, who shared their joys and griefs with him. Lansbury wrote of them:

> Whatever future there may be for me, my most cherished
> memories will be of the long, long years of work and pleasure,

agitation and propaganda, carried on in company with these countless numbers of people, most of whom possess no money, no property, but who do possess the greatest of God's gifts to man, the spirit of comradeship and loyalty to each other . . .[48]

Lansbury's fraternity did not find an outlet in hearty get-togethers in the Commons' bars. It was rather expressed in his kindness, graciousness and concern for others. There are many examples of his kindness to fellow socialists. In 1917, when the revolutionary Scottish socialist, John MacLean, lay seriously ill in prison, Lansbury wrote to Lloyd George appealing for clemency, offering to take him away to recuperate, and observing that MacLean 'had many of the radical characteristics which Lloyd George would recognise in himself'.[49] MacLean was released and Lansbury arranged for him to rest in Hastings. His kindness was expressed not just to prominent socialists but to all who needed it. Penniless political refugees, men seeking work, women striving to avoid the workhouse, his big heart was open to them all. As Laski wrote:

I wish I knew how to measure his innumerable kindness to every sort and kind of person. George Lansbury has never sent a man or woman away without a hearing; and he has never failed to try and do his best for every applicant. No one whom he has helped has ever been humiliated by the way in which he has played the generous part.[50]

They never felt humiliated for Lansbury possessed the quality of graciousness. George Thomas recalled that, when Lansbury stayed at his home, his elderly mother appreciated the humility, considerateness and graciousness of the Labour leader. It was noticed also by a Mrs Ursula Roberts who observed Lansbury at a conference where he underwent savage heckling and abuse for his pacifist views. In a letter, now in the Lansbury Collection, she recorded that he remained 'uniformly gentle and courteous'. She continued that later:

I found myself asking him to say a prayer for me. At once he bowed his head and prayed silently. All the weekend he was kind to me and quietly considerate. I was deeply drawn to him.

Even during the months he spent in the Manor Hospital in Golders Green, following his fall, and even when spending his last days there, Lansbury displayed an interest in and concern for the hospital staff. John Postgate entered the same hospital for an operation in 1950 and noted that his grandfather 'was still remembered with great affection by the older staff, the surgeon-in-chief and many others'.[51]

Lansbury's kindness, graciousness and singular concern did stimulate in many people what Raymond Postgate called 'an affection whose quality and extent cannot even be explained to those who did not see it and remember it'.[52] The outcome was that Lansbury forged many friendships with people whom he saw frequently and a sense of continuing fraternity with some whom he saw only occasionally. This fraternity, his practice of equality and his integrity make him the outstanding socialist practitioner of his era.

This chapter has said much in appreciation of George Lansbury. One reason for so doing is that he now receives little attention even in books about socialist figures. For example, Kenneth Morgan's well received study of Labour leaders has no place for him.[53] Another reason is that when recent text books do mention him, they tend to focus only on the last years of his life and depict him, in Seaman's words, as 'elderly, benevolent and harmless' and not as a serious political figure.[54]

In attempting to correct the neglect and misrepresentation of Lansbury, it is important not to overstate his prominence and virtues. In the inter-war years, the Labour Party was strengthened by a reorganization of its administration and by increasing support from the trade union movement. Lansbury played little part in these developments. He was not a noted policy maker on the party's national executive. Indeed, in his early years in parliament and during his editorship of the *Herald*, some Labour stalwarts considered him too far removed from official policy. Further, his political misjudgments and personal failings should not be ignored. He erred in 1912 when he resigned a seat which he thought he would regain in a by-election. Later he may well have been mistaken in advising Labour to form minority governments. As a journalist, in his attempt to counter the British public's negative views about events in Soviet Russia, he did present too rosy a picture of what was happening there. At the end, he overestimated the effect he could have on men like Hitler and Mussolini. As a resident of Poplar who kept open house, he did at times, as Edgar reveals, get 'irritated beyond words'.[55]

Yet these limitations are dwarfed by Lansbury's abilities, character and achievements. This biography has tried to show that he was not just a long-living socialist whose life span covered the history of the Labour Party from its birth to forming a government but also that he was one of its greatest figures. He became a prophet of socialism who proclaimed its message in print and spoken word; who convinced many that socialism and Christianity went together; who encouraged countless individuals in their commitment to socialism. He was a socialist participant who ably filled many posts, any one of which would have taxed most people. Amongst these posts was that of leader of the party after its shattering defeat in 1931 when, of all its remaining MPs, he was credited with doing most to reconstruct and perhaps to save the parliamentary Labour Party. Not least, he was a socialist practitioner who demonstrated that socialism was not just a political activity performed in the Commons or the council chamber, not just a hoped-for utopia in some distant future, but was a life to be lived in the present. As Lord Tonypandy, the former George Thomas, put it, 'Britain is richer because he lived.'

References

1   W. Lax, *Lax His Book*, Epworth Press, 1937, p. 291.

2   G. Lansbury, *My England*, Selwyn and Blount Ltd, 1934, p. 23.

3   Ibid., p. 16.

4   Ibid., p. 209.

5   G. Foote, *The Labour Party's Political Thought. A History*, Croom Helm, 1985, pp. 32–36.

6   H. Laski, Introduction to G. Lansbury, *My Life*, Constable & Co., Ltd., reprinted 1931, p. x.

7   N. Dennis & A.H. Halsey, *English Ethical Socialism*, Clarendon Press, 1988, pp. 4–8.

8   G. Lansbury, Foreword to *Unemployment and Opportunity: Some Practical Suggestions*, National Council of Social Service, undated.

9   Lansbury, *My England*, p. 48.

10   Ibid., p. 71.

11   Ibid., p. 111.

12   Ibid., p. 15.

13   Cited by E. Lansbury, *George Lansbury, My Father*, Sampson, Marston & Co., 1934, p. 7.

14   G. Lansbury, chapter in G. Haw (ed), *Christianity and the Working Classes*, Macmillan & Co., 1906, pp. 176–77.

15   R. Postgate, *The Life of George Lansbury*, Longmans, Green & Co., 1951, p. 57.

16   Lansbury, *My England*, p. 236.

17   Laski, Introduction to G. Lansbury, p. x.

18   G. Lansbury, *Looking Backwards And Forewards*, Blackie and Son, 1935, p. 243.

19   Cited by E. Lansbury, *George Lansbury, My Father*, p. 160.

20   Lansbury, *My England*, p. 32.

21   Ibid., pp. 36–37.

22   Ibid., p. 38.

23   J. Simmons, *Soap-Box Evangelist*, Janay Publishing Co., 1971, p. 12.

24   Cited by St. J. Groser, *Politics and Persons*. SCM Press, 1949, p. 24.

25   Cited by Postgate, *Life of George Lansbury*, p. 56.

26   E. Norman, *The Victorian Christian Socialists*, Cambridge University Press, 1987, p. 17.

27   See R. Terrill, *R. H. Tawney & His Times*, André Deutsch, 1974.

28   Postgate, *Life of George Lansbury*, p. 293.

29   Lansbury, *My England*, p. 240.

30   Laski, Introduction to G. Lansbury, p. xi.

31   Simmons, *Soap-Box Evangelist*, p. 119.

32   Laski, Introduction to G. Lansbury, p. xiii.

33   Letter from Rev. Allan Harling to the author.

34   N. Mitchison, *You May Well Ask*, Flamingo, 1979, p. 185.

35   Laski, Introduction to G. Lansbury, p. xii.

36   G. Armstrong (ed.), *London's Struggle for Socialism 1848–1948*, Thames Publications, 1948, p. 43.

37   Geoffrey Goodman, letter to the author.

[38] Professor John Postgate, letter to the author.

[39] A.J.P. Taylor, *English History 1914–1945*, Penguin Books, reprinted 1987, p. 142.

[40] H. Hyndman, *Further Reminiscences*, Macmillan & Co., 1912, p. 283.

[41] G. Lansbury, *My Life*, Constable & Co., 1928, p. 3.

[42] E. Lansbury, *George Lansbury, My Father*, pp. 20–21.

[43] St. J. Groser, *Politics and Persons*, pp. 22–23.

[44] F. Field, *Losing Out*, Basil Blackwell, 1989, p. 155.

[45] F. Gibbons, *There's A Divinity*, private publication, 1988, p. 22.

[46] E. Lansbury, *George Lansbury, My Father*, p. 17.

[47] Lansbury, *Looking Backwards*, p. 234.

[48] Lansbury, *My Life*, p. 265.

[49] B. Ripley & J. McHugh, *J. MacLean*, Manchester University Press, 1989, p. 101.

[50] Laski, Introduction to G. Lansbury, p. ii.

[51] Professor John Postgate, letter to the author.

[52] Postgate, *Life of George Lansbury*, p. 44.

[53] K. Morgan, *Labour People*, Oxford University Press, 1987.

[54] L.C.B. Seaman, *Post Victorian Britain 1920–1951*, Methuen & Co. Ltd., 1966, p. 206.

[55] E. Lansbury, *George Lansbury, My Father*, p. 66.

PERSONAL POSTSCRIPT

A main reason for writing this book has been to bring Lansbury back to public recognition. In addition, I have written it because Lansbury, although I never met him, has been a strong influence on my life.

I was born and bred in Ilford, near Bow. My paternal grandfather, a bricklayer, was an active trade unionist and Labour supporter. Our family took the *Daily Herald*. Not surprisingly, I have always had some vague knowledge about 'Good old George'. However, not until adulthood did I come across a copy of Postgate's out-of-print *Life of George Lansbury*. This stimulated me to trace and read Lansbury's own books, which subsequently strongly affected my life in two major spheres: my Christian faith and my involvement in local neighbourhoods.

During the 1960s, I experienced some disillusionment with both the church and the Labour Party. Dwelling in Birmingham in the era of Enoch Powell's 'rivers of blood' speech, I was dismayed to perceive that some church members, far from opposing racism, actually supported it. I also observed Christians content to enjoy their own affluence while ignoring the needs of thousands of fellow citizens who were in poverty. Such factors weakened my faith and could have driven me even more fully into party politics. However, I was also troubled by developments within the Labour Party. The acquisitiveness, high incomes and naked careerism of some of its leading figures seemed in direct contradiction to the socialist aim of equality. Further, I disliked much of the war-like factionalism which seemed at odds with the concept of fraternity. In short, I was having doubts about my allegiance both to the church and the Labour Party and also wondering if membership of one was inconsistent with membership of the other.

Eventually, on rereading the Bible, I established to my own

satisfaction that, whatever the failings of parts of the church, Christianity is a religion with a concern for the oppressed, particularly those oppressed by social deprivations. In the Old Testament, I read of a God who condemned low wages, money-lenders and poverty and who ordained laws to redistribute property and wealth. In the New Testament, I read of a Christ who chose to dwell with powerless people, who stood up to those in high positions, who attacked the rich who would not share their goods and who called them to give up their affluence and to follow him. I became convinced that Christianity was about both forming a personal relationship with God and about striving to form a just society on earth.

Soon after, I discovered Lansbury, who proclaimed a socialism which was about aiming for the structural reforms to promote equality, about strong bonds of concern and love between socialists, and about putting socialist principles into practice in our everyday behaviour and relationships. He reaffirmed my belief not in socialism, for I had never lost that, but in the Labour Party as the vehicle for achieving and expressing it. Simultaneously, I read that Lansbury too had gone through a period of doubts as to whether Christianity and socialism were reconcilable and had endured a time of alienation from the church. I became convinced by his reasoning that Christianity and socialism were not the same but that they should be related. He argued powerfully that the Christian concept of love for one's neighbour could best be encouraged and promoted within a socialist environment. Lansbury reached a destination where he could live as a Christian and as a socialist. I have come the same way and Lansbury's words and example have helped me to get there.

My working life has been spent in the world of welfare. After a period as a local authority child care officer and several years in academic posts, I worked for over a decade in a community project run by the Children's Society. In recent years I have been with a small, neighbourhood project in Easterhouse, Glasgow. My experience is thus not in the large-scale social services of income maintenance or housing but in what are now called the personal social services and local community services. Undoubtedly, these services have helped many citizens yet they have been subject to fierce criticism. For instance, Professor Hadley and his colleagues attacked them for being too bureaucratic, too centralized, too remote from users, and too dominated by professionals. In particular, they castigated services for casting users into the role of 'passive consumers' who had little say and no control over the agencies which were supposed to help them.[1] Like many other project workers, I have had to face up to these criticisms and also grapple with other issues such as the role of voluntary societies in areas of social deprivation, who should run them, and the lifestyle of their staff.

Once again, I have been stimulated by the insights articulated by Lansbury. Of course, the welfare and community provision of his day was not as extensive as that of today. Yet he participated in much welfare activity. He saw many of the responsibilities of the Poor Law taken over by central and local authorities. He observed central government trying to intervene in 'distressed areas'. He had intimate knowledge of the many voluntary bodies, large and small, which abounded in the East End.

Lansbury's major criticism of the social services, particularly those based on neighbourhoods known to him, was that, for all their good intentions, they were frequently dominated by and served the interests of the middle-class people who ran them. He displayed much hostility towards Toynbee Hall, the settlement which served as a base for many privileged people to do their social work in the East End. In *My Life*, Lansbury launched a sustained attack which included the judgment that:

> my sixty years' experience in East London leaves me quite
> unable to discover what permanent social influence Toynbee
> Hall or any other settlement has had on the life and labour of
> the people.[2]

Lansbury's attack was resented by Clara Grant, the long-serving school teacher in the area. In a small book, she pointed to the many services and people Toynbee Hall had brought to the area.[3] However, she misunderstood the nature of Lansbury's analysis. He admired and welcomed outsiders who gave themselves to the East End and Clara Grant herself was one to whom he paid tribute. He certainly believed that statutory bodies should be the main providers of basic social needs such as housing, income, health care and education but he also worked with and encouraged a number of voluntary agencies. He went out of his way to praise Mary Hughes, who ran a project called the Dew Drop Inn in Whitechapel. He wrote that she:

literally believes the teachings of Jesus and is fine enough in character to strive to live her ideals . . . Mary Hughes and her little Dew Drop Inn will never become famous as Toynbee Hall is famous: she trains no clever persons to become governors, cabinet ministers or members of parliament, but in the days to come her life and work will prove more lasting than any of the others I have mentioned, because she lives with the people, sharing their sorrows and joys. For her there is no separate house with parlours: her idea of mixing of the classes is to live together as men and women.[4]

Lansbury's applause of Mary Hughes indicates that he was not opposed to all voluntary bodies. It is worth interjecting here that the present Toynbee Hall and the settlement movement in general is now much more radical than in Lansbury's day. However, in his time he perceived much that he considered harmful in the larger voluntary agencies. Four criticisms — which he acknowledged could also apply to some state services — stand out.

First, the staff and supporters of such organizations often separated themselves from the residents of the areas they said they wanted to help. Unlike Mary Hughes they did not share their lives, themselves, their homes with other residents. Instead, by their large incomes, their mode of dress, their lifestyle, they accentuated rather than lessened the differences between rich and poor.

Second, Lansbury observed that some of the young men and women from 'good schools' who came to the East End to voice their concern about poverty were really using the poor for their own future advancement. They did not stay and, he declared, the knowledge they acquired from mixing with socially deprived people 'is later on used to secure for them first-class positions as Government or municipal servants'.[5]

Third, Lansbury noted that the same people, who once called for 'a complete social revolution' to abolish poverty and class distinctions, lost their ardour when, 'like the rich young man in the parable', they realized that such changes would abolish their own high status and incomes. They then contented themselves with much reduced objectives such as 'the business of making the present conditions more tolerable'.[6] Again, as he wrote 'My disagreement with them is that they appear to desire a change in social conditions, but wish, at the same time, to maintain their positions in life as now.'[7]

Fourth, Lansbury saw that such organizations, whether they be large voluntary societies set up by the affluent or Special Areas Committees imposed by the government, did not belong to the people of the East End. The residents of Bow, Poplar and Whitechapel might clean Toynbee Hall, might wait at its tables, might even benefit from its clubs and classes. But they did not own or control it. Such agencies belonged to the expanding empires of outside organizations and hence served the interests of the middle-class and professional people who dominated their committees and held the leading jobs. Whatever the immediate relief given by some of the services, the agencies maintained existing social structures with their own people remaining in the superior and local residents in the inferior positions.

Given his strictures about many affluent, middle-class people who were keen to be involved in social agencies, what did Lansbury see as their role? For a start, he told them that giving donations to good causes was not sufficient. Postgate recorded that:

> he thanked them warmly for their generosity, but reminded
> them that they had no right to the money in the first place,
> and that they would never be at ease until they gave personal
> service to the cause as well as all the money they could spare.[8]

Giving 'personal service' meant, as he explained in *Your Part in Poverty*, that they should 'get into the working-class movement'.[9] They should be prepared to serve others, to work and live alongside those in need and to cede leadership to working-class residents.

In his area, Lansbury wanted services in which a major part was played by the ordinary residents of the East End. He possessed a genuine faith in the abilities and qualities of working-class people. As early as 1894, in a letter to the *Star* of 25 January, he wrote, 'If the workers are ever to be raised or to raise themselves it must be by appealing to the very best that is in them rather than in the worst.' He meant that the appeal should not be for them to use violence but rather to their capacities to do the jobs and make the decisions usually considered the preserve of the middle class. He believed that the kind of people he mixed with were the ones best equipped to organize the services — and industries — which affected their lives. As time went on, he witnessed the residents of Poplar making a success of administering the Poor Law and the borough council. Such faith stayed with him until the end of his days and in *My England* he reaffirmed that 'we, the ordinary people, hewers of wood and drawers of water, possess the power to build the Socialist State and to build it now'.[10] One way of building that state was for these people to run the voluntary and statutory services that could do so much to improve the quality of life. For they understood the needs of people like themselves and they were capable of maintaining services without maintaining the social class differences which underpin inequality.

It seems to me that Lansbury's criticisms and analyses of social services are still pertinent today. The idea that services and projects should be controlled by residents from the areas where they are located, and that many of their staff should be locally recruited, has much to commend it. The principle that Lansbury demonstrated in his life, of not seeking to enrich himself, of continuing to identify with the ordinary people whom he wished to serve, and continuing to treat them with respect as equal human beings are still goals to be sought. Within my own sphere I know that if they are attained they will help promote the kind of neighbourhoods and the kind of society characterized by the equality, the fraternity and the love which were so near to the heart of Good old George.

References

1   R. Hadley & S. Hatch, *Social Welfare and the Failure of the State*, Allen and Unwin, 1981.

2   G. Lansbury, *My Life*, Constable, 1928, p. 131.

3   C. Grant, *From Me to We*, Fern Street Settlement, 1940, pp. 37–38.

4   Lansbury, *My Life*, p. 131.

5   G. Lansbury, *Your Part In Poverty*, The Herald, 1917, p. 91.

6   Lansbury, *Your Part In Poverty*, p. 91.

7   G. Lansbury, *These Things Shall Be*, Swarthmore Press, 1920, p. 46.

8   R. Postgate, *The Life of George Lansbury*, Longmans, Green & Co., 1951, p. 182.

9   Lansbury, *Your Part In Poverty*, p. 108.

10 G. Lansbury, *My England*, Selwyn and Blount Ltd., 1934, p. 253.

BIBLIOGRAPHY

Published Sources

G. Armstrong (ed.), *London's Struggle for Socialism 1848–1948*, Thames Publications, 1948.

C. Attlee, *The Labour Party in Perspective*, Gollancz, 1937.

Mrs Barnardo and J. Marchant, *Memoirs of the Late Dr Barnardo*, Hodder and Stoughton, 1907.

M. Bondfield, *A Life's Work*, Hutchinson & Co., 1948.

N. Branson, *Poplarism 1919–1925*, Lawrence Wishart, 1979.

V. Brittain, *Testament of Experience*, Fontana Paperbacks, 1980.

F. Brockway, *Bermondsey Story. The Life of Alfred Salter*, Allen and Unwin, 1949.

G. Brown, *Maxton*, Mainstream Publishing, 1986.

M. Ceadle, *Pacifism in Britain 1914–1945*, Clarendon Press, 1980.

M. Cole, *Beatrice Webb*, Longmans, Green & Co., second edition, 1946.

M. Cowling, *The Impact of Labour 1920–1924*, Cambridge University Press, 1971.

M. A. Crowther, *The Workhouse System 1834–1929*, Batsford Academic, 1981.

N. Dennis and A.H. Halsey, *English Ethical Socialism*, Clarendon Press, 1988.

M. Fels, *The Life of Joseph Fels*, Doubleday, Doran & Co., 1940.

F. Field, *Losing Out*, Basil Blackwell, 1989.

W. Fishman, *East End 1888*, Duckworth, 1988.

M. Foot, *Aneurin Bevan*, vol. 1, Paladin Granada, 1975.

M. Foot, 'Ideals and Raw Deals', *Guardian*, 10 April 1987.

G. Foote, *The Labour Party's Political Thought: A History*, Croom Helm, 1985.

F. Gibbons, *There's A Divinity*, private publication, 1988.

C. Grant, *From Me to We*, Fern Street Settlement, 1940.

St J. Groser, *Politics and Persons*, SCM Press, 1949.

R. Hadley and S. Hatch, *Social Welfare and the Failure of the State*, Allen and Unwin, 1981.

W. Hannington, *Black Coffins and the Unemployed*, Fact Books, 1939.

G. Haw, *From Workhouse to Westminster: The Life Story of Will Crooks*, Cassell & Co., 1907.

J. Heywood, *Children in Care*, Routledge and Kegan Paul, 1959.

C. Hill, *Lenin and the Russian Revolution*, 4th impression, English Universities Press, 1957.

B. Holman, *Putting Families First*, Macmillan Education, 1988.

H. Hyndman, *Further Reminiscences*, Macmillan & Co., 1912.

S. Koss, *The Rise and Fall of the Political Press in Britain*, vol. 2, Hamish Hamilton, 1984.

E. Lansbury, *George Lansbury, My Father*, Sampson Low, Marston & Co., 1934.

G. Lansbury, foreword to *Unemployment and Opportunity: Some Practical Suggestions*, National Council of Social Service, Undated.

G. Lansbury, *Looking Backwards and Forwards*, Blackie and Son, 1935.

G. Lansbury, *My England*, Selwyn and Blount Ltd., 1934.

G. Lansbury, *My Life*, Constable, 1928.

G. Lansbury, *My Quest for Peace*, Michael Joseph Ltd., 1938.

G. Lansbury, *The Miracle of Fleet Street*, Victoria House and Labour Publishing Co., 1925.

G. Lansbury, *These Things Shall Be*, Swarthmore Press, 1920.

G. Lansbury, *What I Saw In Russia*, Leonard Parsons, 1920.

G. Lansbury, *Your Part in Poverty*, The Herald, 1917.

G. Lansbury, chapter in G. Haw (ed.), *Christianity and the Working Classes*, Macmillan & Co., 1906.

V. Lansbury, *An Englishwoman in the USSR*, Putman, 1940.

H. Laski, Introduction to G. Lansbury, *My Life*, reissued 1931.

W. Lax, *Lax His Book*, The Epworth Press, 1937.

H. Lees-Smith (ed.), *Encyclopaedia of the Labour Movement*, vol. 2, Caxton Publishing Co., 1924.

J. G. Lockhart, *Cosmo Gordon Lang*, Hodder and Stoughton, 1949.

S. Mayor, *The Churches and the Labour Movement*, Independent Press, 1967.

R. McKibbon, *The Evolution of the Labour Party, 1910–1924*, Oxford University Press, 1974.

I. McLean, *Keir Hardie*, Allen Lane, 1975.

J. McNair, *James Maxton*, Allen and Unwin, 1955.

H. McShane and J. Smith, *No Mean Fighter*, Pluto Press, 1978.

N. Middleton, *When Family Failed*, Gollancz, 1971.

N. Mitchison, *You May Well Ask*, Flamingo, 1979.

B. Moore, *All Out*, Sheffield City Libraries, 1985.

A. Morgan, *J. Ramsay MacDonald*, Manchester University Press, 1987.

K. Morgan, *Labour People*, Oxford University Press, 1987.

S. Morrison, *I Renounce War: the Story of the Peace Pledge Union*, Sheppard Press, 1962.

O. Mosley, *My Life*, Nelson, 1968.

E. Norman, *The Victorian Christian Socialists*, Cambridge University Press, 1987.

S. Pankhurst, *The Suffragette Movement*, Virago, 1978.

H. Pelling, 'Governing Without Power', *Political Quarterly*, vol. xxxii, 1961.

B. Pimlott, *Hugh Dalton*, Cape, 1985.

J. Pimlott, *Toynbee Hall*, Dent & Co., 1935.

Poor Law Minority Report. Report of Debate Between George Lansbury and H. Quelch, The Twentieth Century Press Ltd., 1910.

R. Postgate, *The Life of George Lansbury*, Longmans, Green & Co., 1951.

B. Ripley and J. McHugh, *J. MacLean*, Manchester University Press, 1989.

P. Romero, *E. Sylvia Pankhurst*, Yale University Press, 1987.

Royal Commission on the Poor Law and the Relief of Distress, HMSO, 1909.

P. Ryan, 'Poplarism 1894–1930', in P. Thane (ed.), *The Origins of British Social Policy*, Croom Helm, 1978.

L.C.B. Seaman, *Post Victorian Britain*, Methuen & Co. Ltd., 1966.

E. Shinwell, *I've Lived Through It All*, Gollancz Ltd., 1973.

J. Simmons, *Soap-Box Evangelist*, Janay Publishing Co., 1972.

A.J.P. Taylor, *English History 1914–1945*, Penguin Books, reprinted 1987.

R. Terrill, *R.H. Tawney & His Times*, André Deutsch, 1974.

D. Thomson, *England in the Twentieth Century*, Jonathan Cape, 1964.

S. Webb, 'The First Labour Government', *Political Quarterly*, vol. xxxii, 1961.

Unpublished Sources

Rev. Clive Barrett, letter to the author, 29 November 1988.

Professor William Fishman, letter to the author, 2 October 1989.

Professor William Fishman, recorded interview with the author, London, 9 November 1989.

Mr Michael Foot MP, recorded interview with the author, London, 13 May 1988.

Mr Geoffrey Goodman, letter to the author, 16 November 1989.

Rev. Allan Harling, letter to the author, 17 May 1989.

Mr Terry Lansbury, letter to the author, 5 September 1989.

Mrs Marjorie Pinhorn, letter to the author, 16 August 1989.

Mr Richmond Postgate, letter to the author, 24 February 1987.

Professor John Postgate, letter to the author, 9 August 1989.

Mrs Rose Rosamund, letter to the author, 22 July 1989.

Lord Soper, recorded interview with the author, London, 12 July 1988.

Viscount Tonypandy, recorded interview with the author, Musselborough, 30 April 1988.

Mrs Esme Whiskin, letter to the author, 21 August 1989.

Mrs G. Wootton, letter to the author, 2 August 1989.

Archives

Lansbury's personal papers are lodged with the London School of Economics where they are known as the Lansbury Collection. They consist of a large collection of letters to and by Lansbury, notes on speeches he gave, papers he received for meetings, and many reports about him in newspapers. The Bancroft Road Library in Tower Hamlets possesses a smaller collection but it also holds many of his books and pamphlets.

INDEX